ANTHEM CRITICAL THINKING AND WRITING SKILLS

ANTHEM CRITICAL THINKING AND WRITING SKILLS

An Introductory Guide

VICTORIA PONTZER EHRHARDT, PhD

Anthem Press
An imprint of Wimbledon Publishing Company
www.anthempress.com

This edition first published in UK and USA 2011
by ANTHEM PRESS
75-76 Blackfriars Road, London SE1 8HA, UK
or PO Box 9779, London SW19 7ZG, UK
and
244 Madison Ave. #116, New York, NY 10016, USA

Copyright © Victoria Pontzer Ehrhardt 2011

The author asserts the moral right to be identified as the author of this work.

"Love is a Fallacy" © 1941 by Max Shulman, renewed 1979.
Reprinted by permission of the Harold Matson Co., Inc., New York.

All rights reserved. Without limiting the rights under copyright reserved above,
no part of this publication may be reproduced, stored or introduced into
a retrieval system, or transmitted, in any form or by any means
(electronic, mechanical, photocopying, recording or otherwise),
without the prior written permission of both the copyright
owner and the above publisher of this book.

British Library Cataloguing-in-Publication Data
A catalogue record for this book is available from the British Library.

Library of Congress Cataloging-in-Publication Data
Ehrhardt, Victoria Pontzer.
 Anthem critical thinking and writing skills : an introductory guide / Victoria Pontzer Ehrhardt.
   p. cm. – (Anthem learning)
 Includes index.
  ISBN 978-1-84331-870-5 (pbk.)
  1. English language–Composition and exercises–Study and teaching (Secondary)
  2. English language–Rhetoric–Study and teaching (Higher)
  3. Critical thinking–Study and teaching (Secondary)
  4. Critical thinking–Study and teaching (Higher) I. Title.
 LB1631.E475 2011
 808'.042071–dc23
                    2011039754

ISBN-13: 978 1 84331 870 5 (Pbk)
ISBN-10: 1 84331 870 9 (Pbk)

This title is also available as an eBook.

CONTENTS

1 Introduction to Critical Thinking 1
   Critical Thinking: The Human Mind at Work 1
   Warm-up Activities 3
   Metacognition 6

2 What Is Argument? 9
   Defining Argument and Debate 9
   Can Any Point Be Argued? 9
   How Does an Argument Develop? 10
   Developing an Argument 11
   The Proposition 12
   Practice Exercises on Propositions 16
   Major and Minor Propositions 17
   Chapter Review 19

3 Research and Gathering Evidence 21
   Gathering Evidence 21
   Evaluating Evidence 23
   Using Peer-Reviewed Sources 25
   Recognizing Bad Evidence 25
   The Next Step: Organizing Evidence 28
   Practice Exercises in Gathering Evidence 29
   Chapter Review 30

4 Inductive Reasoning 31
   Generalization 31
   The Analogy 33

Practice in Analogies   34
Analogy, Metaphor and Simile   34
Chapter Review   35

5 Deductive Reasoning   37
Thinking by Classifying: Venn Diagrams   37
Reasoning by Classification: The Syllogism   40
Using Venn Diagrams to Understand the Syllogism   41
Working with the Syllogism without Diagrams   46
"Jabberwocky" and the Ultimate Syllogism Practice   52
Syllogisms and Political Arguments   55
Reasoning by Either/Or   56
Reasoning by If/Then   58
Chapter Review   58

6 Errors in Reasoning: The Classical Fallacies   61
Classical Fallacies of Processing Information   62
Classical Fallacies about People and Personalities   68

7 Reasoning through the Ages   73
The Context of Argument: Logos, Ethos and Pathos   73
The Context of Argument: Two Modern Approaches   74
The Context of Argument: A Literary Approach   75
  "Love is a Fallacy" by Max Shulman   76
  Persuasion in Poetry   86

8 Putting It All Together: A Research Project   93
Selecting a Topic and Forming a Proposition   93
Gathering, Evaluating and Organizing Evidence   97
Writing, Citing and Editing   102
Checklist for the Persuasive Research Paper   104
Chapter Review   105
All in a Day's Work   105

Appendix 1   Answers for Practice Exercises and Chapter Reviews   107

Appendix 2   Logic Test   119

Appendix 3   Answers to Logic Test   123

Appendix 4   Persuasive Research Paper Rubric   127

Index   129

INTRODUCTION TO CRITICAL THINKING

Critical Thinking: The Human Mind at Work

Critical thinking skills reveal our minds at work. Daily life, education and career activities involve looking at information, evaluating the information and making choices.

Every day, we decide. We evaluate. We work with our family, our team and our co-workers to find the best idea, to make the right decision, to select the best course of action. Often, we observe, evaluate and decide subconsciously. How does that happen?

The answer is that the human mind is wired to reason. The goal of this book is to bring awareness to these aspects of reasoning: observation, evaluation and decision making. Critical thinking happens best when we plan to put our natural thinking abilities to their clearest use.

The human mind is programmed to think logically. One can observe this in the youngest infant. Infants realize quickly, although subconsciously, "When I cry, they pick me up." The baby has used "Cause and Effect" thinking at only a few weeks old. The new parents likewise use the same thinking skills, adding in the components of observation and examining possibilities. Is the baby hungry? Does its diaper need to be changed? For thousands of years, mothers have instinctively nurtured their infants' growing minds along with their bodies. Before actual conversation is possible, the parent and infant are using thinking skills to problem-solve as parents encourage infants to thrive.

Soon, that infant will be crawling, then walking and starting to talk. How often have we seen parents panic as they teach their toddler his or her first words? After "Mama" and "Papa," the toddler may learn a word for a family pet. "Kitty" the parents say, and the little one says, "kitty." But no sooner is that word learned, than a dog comes into view. The worried parents may wonder, "How will I teach him that it's a doggie?"

Within a few months, the toddler has the difference between a "kitty" and a "doggie" all worked out. In fact, the child's mind can work out a very complicated application of this very problem, working through the process of observation and categorization. A 3-year-old can realize that a large collie and a low-to-the-ground dachshund are both dogs and that Aunt Jane's pet is a cat. An infant's mind recognizes groups, patterns and commonalities, and then makes predictions based on those concepts. That's logic.

What happens in the reasoning process? It works like this:

The human mind has an innate capacity to remember and then to process. We recognize groups, patterns and commonalities, and we make predictions based on those concepts.

A no is as good as a yes. Yes, that item belongs to the group. No, that one doesn't. The mind sees the details of what belongs and what doesn't. We see details, we remember, we categorize and then we make the mental move to a new, named idea.

That is the basic reasoning process.

Throughout the ages, great thinkers have talked, written and investigated the way we reason. Perhaps the most notable of these great thinkers is Aristotle, who observed and recorded his observations about the human mind at work. The logic and reasoning skills taught in this book are based on Aristotelian logic. In the twentieth century, two Western thinkers, the psychologist Carl R. Rogers and philosopher Stephen Toulmin, created their own models of reasoning and debate. Each created a framework that was thought to be especially appropriate for topics of modern social, political and personal decision making. More about Rogerian argument and the Toulmin model can be found in Chapter 7.

Other twentieth- and twenty-first century scholars have expanded our understanding of how language shapes our thoughts. We now know that language and ideas are closely related. Using language rather than number logic to process ideas is a purposeful part of the reasoning process. Words identify ideas.

For the human mind, there is something special about any "idea." It is not enough to have the idea; we want to share, to convince. That is what this book is about. By taking a step-by-step approach to the reasoning process, anyone can take the innate thinking skills that come naturally to them and hone those skills to become a strong evaluator of their own opinions and those of others.

The practiced thinker can recognize weak arguments, and values strong, well-reasoned ideas. Using thinking skills in a purposeful manner gives people at work or at school the persuasive powers to convince others to see their point of view.

- It might be a casual decision – we might want to encourage our group of friends to see a particular film or go to a particular restaurant for dinner.
- In a more serious vein, we may want to convince friends and family to support a certain candidate in the next election.
- For social plans or for serious decisions, a study of language and logic can help us sharpen our decision-making abilities and our persuasive skills.

Warm-up Activities

Throughout the chapters of this text, readers will be exercising an important part of the body: the brain. We will follow the plan of other exercise regimens and start by warming up with three thinking challenges. These practice exercise and reinforce three mental habits:

1. Flexibility: Encouraging our mind to bend around ideas allows us to look about for inspiration. Rather than providing ideas from the outside, Practice 1.a encourages us to look around inside our own storehouse of vocabulary and ideas.

2. Organization: Organization starts with identifying certain characteristics like size and function. The next, seemingly automatic step is grouping together items with similar characteristics. Since it is easier to organize three-dimensional objects and much harder to organize ideas, we start our practice with everyday items like clothing and eating utensils.

3. Processing: Reasoning, deciding, selecting, evaluating – these are all mental processes. A mental process is a movement of ideas, where given information is moved to a new place, a solution. We will work with some processing games, often called brainteasers, to encourage our mind to move the given set of information through to an answer.

All of these challenges can be done on your own or in a group.

Practice 1.a. Flexibility with language: The "Magic 8" challenge

Mr Lee attended a program led by a motivational speaker who encouraged the audience to follow the "Eight Magic Ates" to have a good life. When he returned home, Mr Lee could only remember four of the speaker's "Ates." Here are the words Mr Lee remembers:

    Anticipate   Cooperate   Create   Integrate

Your challenge is to "brainstorm" and come up with as many words ending in "ate" as you can. If you are working in a group, share the lists and create one large list with each word included once. After you have created a large list, select the "Magic 8" that you think are the best ones to follow in everyday life.

Upon completion of this practice, your mind has accomplished several things: first, you had to delve into your own storehouse of vocabulary to find additional words that end in "ate." Next, you had to review the meanings of each word, and evaluate the concept for which each word stands. Then, you had to downsize a list that you had just expanded. That is the flexibility exercise: make it larger, then make it smaller. Moving from step to step in this activity encourages mental flexibility.

Practice 1.b. Organization challenge

On an unlined piece of paper, draw a picture of a tall chest of drawers. Imagine filling the chest with your own clothes. You have socks and undergarments, T-shirts, jeans or slacks and a few heavier pieces of clothing for inclement weather. On your simple drawing of this chest of drawers, label the drawers to show where you would put your clothes.

What did you decide? Are your socks in one of the top drawers? Underclothes near the top? Shirts in the middle? Heavier clothing at the bottom? If you are working in a group setting, compare your answers with others. You will find that most of your "labels" match the other folks who try this.

Furniture makers have known this for centuries. There is a quiet understanding that people like to sort and organize their belongings. That is why an antique bureau will hold clothing in much the same way as a modern chest from Ikea.

We can recognize our human tendency to organize objects by size and use. Move on to the next organization challenge.

Practice 1.c. Organization challenge

On another piece of unlined paper, create a simple diagram of a wall of kitchen cabinets. Imagine that you have just moved into a new house and you must unpack kitchenware and put it in the cabinets. Label the cabinets and drawers to show where you would put glasses, dishes, silverware, pots and pans, and cleaning products.

Compare your choices with a team member. Again, you will see that most people reveal a common pattern: glasses and dishes in the top cabinets, silverware in the drawers and cleaning products under the sink. Even if you don't agree 100%, ask a team member if they would ever put the glasses or dishes under the sink. Most respondents will prefer to put only cleaning products and objects that do not hold food in the area directly under the sink.

Perhaps you knew that you were already very careful about organizing your clothing, home and hobby items. Alternately, you might be the person who thought your organizational skills were lacking. Even those who think they are not organized by nature realize, after completing these two exercises, that they do possess certain innate organization skills.

Reinforcing our ability to organize objects is a starter skill in strong critical thinking. Organizing abstract ideas is a more advanced skill. As we review our skill in organizing objects, we reinforce the observational and descriptive skills that allow us to organize ideas.

Practice 1.d. Processing skills challenge

In a new language, *teza ylk njym* means "bake berry treats," *alsa entz teza* means "sweet berry muffins" and *rhys ylk alsa* means "bake extra muffins."

With this much information, can you determine how to say "sweet treats" in this language?

  a. *ylk alsa*   c. *njym entz*

  b. *rhys teza*   d. *teza njym*

Practice 1.e. Processing skills challenge

You have 25 coins that total $1.00 in value. What coins do you have, and how many of each?

Practice 1.f. Processing skills challenge

What will the day after the day after tomorrow be if the day before the day before yesterday was Tuesday?

We often think of processing information in terms of numbers. Only Practice 1.e relies on number values. Practices 1.d and 1.f rely solely on our use of language.

Early in our schooling, we learn to process numbers in mathematic settings. It is important in the field of argument and debate to be able to process words as well.

Metacognition

You can find the solutions to the practice exercises in the appendix at the end of this book. However, it is just as important that you can explain to a classmate, co-worker or friend how you got your answer. After you and a teammate arrive at an answer, explore the answer and ask, "How did you get that?"

You'll notice that the people who problem-solve give different explanations about the thought processes they used when they tried to solve the puzzle.

Some people pick up a pen or pencil. Some start at the end of the idea, some at the beginning. Some people make a drawing or a chart.

To get the answer to the coin challenge (Practice 1.e), you may have written down the value of each coin and added up multiple possibilities. Or you may have actually pulled a few coins out of your pocket to get a visual sense of the problem.

Those explanations tell us how we "think about thinking."

We call this process **metacognition**.

A personal awareness of your own thinking process is an important place to begin the study of logic. Let's give metacognition a try:

First, think about how you started the "translation" problem. Did you use a pencil? Did you draw a diagram? Did you write down the words and cross some of them out?

Next ask, how did you feel? Some responders will say the brainteasers were easy and fun. Some responders feel frustrated. How we react to frustration is a thinking skill in itself.

INTRODUCTION TO CRITICAL THINKING

Our success in finding a solution when we encounter a new mental challenge will be determined by a number of qualities:

- the ability to get started (overcoming inertia)
- a positive response to frustration (it's okay when the first solution doesn't work)
- persistence
- directed questioning
- the ability to quiet background noise
- the quality of wonder and excitement at finding an answer or encountering a new idea

Keep these qualities in mind while you work through the logic skills you are acquiring as you read this text.

Combine how you processed the problem with how you felt when you worked through the puzzle to get an overall view of your analysis skills. Some people have to have pencil and paper; others like to talk it out. Some people will tell you that they just "saw" the answer in their mind, without any words. In the twenty-first century, many students are familiar with the language of thinking; perhaps you already know whether you are a visual or an auditory learner. But it is also important to evaluate your persistence, your response to frustration and the way you "get started" on thinking problems.

Work through the next practice (Practice 1.g) and share your answers with a classmate, friend or partner.

Practice 1.g. Metacognition: Knowing your own mind

Hint: Answer these questions to get in touch with your own, personal thinking style. There are no "right" or "wrong" answers to these questions, but processing the answers is an important step.

1. Do you like to work with a pen/pencil, or just think?
2. When you imagine a solution to a problem, do you picture a solution without any words?
3. Does your anxiety level rise when finding the answer is challenging?

4. Explain this statement: "A no can be as informative as a yes."

5. Do you like to make lists?

6. When you sort through a debatable issue, do you think about the person you will be talking to? Do you imagine talking to that person? Do you ever "argue" into a mirror?

7. Are you easily distracted? Does noise bother you? Or, does a certain amount of background noise/music have a settling effect?

After you have answered the questions about your own thinking habits, share your answers with another person. Overall, you will note similarities in the approach to problem solving, but you will also see small differences. This is important. When we are aware of our own personal pattern of thinking – when we engage in metacognition – and we observe the thinking patterns of others, we move to a new level of respect for critical thinking and for people as thinkers.

Knowing how you think can help you get started. If you know you need a pencil and paper to think, get out the pencil and paper right away. Knowing how you think can put you on the road to refining your thinking process and becoming a first-class critical thinker.

As the title of this book says, we will be looking at critical thinking and writing. We use logic in mathematics and science, of course. Part of the scientific and mathematical process, working through a linear process to a conclusion, will be important. Additionally, we will study the challenges of talking logically, of sharing ideas and convincing others. Our goal is to use logic and language together.

WHAT IS ARGUMENT?

Defining Argument and Debate

What do you picture when you hear the word "argument"? People imagine different scenarios when they hear the word "argument," and many imagine people shouting and looking angry. This is not always the case. In the world of debate, the process of argument is the attempt to persuade another person to accept your views on a debatable subject. The argument itself is both the subject of the debate and the list of reasons that support each side of the debate.

To come to a better understanding of formal argument, debate and the process of persuasion, we will pursue the answers to two defining questions:

1. Can any point be argued?
2. How does an argument develop?

Can Any Point Be Argued?

The short answer is no. Some items are not appropriate topics for argument or debate.

People love to debate. Our most popular and enduring arguments center on issues that we deal with everyday. That is why students debate school rules, community members argue about civic law, professional colleagues argue about conditions in the work place and politicians debate large political issues. In a court of law, lawyers argue for the innocence of their clients.

However, sensible people refrain from arguing about these two things:

1. **Verifiable facts** ("Is New York time 10 hours later than Greenwich Mean Time?")

OR

2. **Matters of taste** ("Tennis is more fun than golf.")

Of course, people do "argue" about those things. Folks sit around the table and insist that chocolate gelato is better than vanilla, or argue about who won last year's World Cup in soccer. But truly, folks will like what they like; we should respect each other's right to enjoy vanilla. As for who won last year's championship – just look it up! Computers and cellular phones have improved most people's ability to find information with ease, limiting the amount of argument we hear about information that can be verified. This is one way that technology has improved our lives.

Vocabulary Note: Take note of the phrases **verifiable facts** and **matters of taste**.

A "verifiable fact" is one that can be checked by going to a reputable source. The source gives us the facts, the data and the dates, in other words, the specific information that makes an argument about that fact, data point or date foolish: we just look it up.

The phrase "matters of taste" identifies personal likes and dislikes, personal selections that are based on very personal feelings about what an individual likes. In this text, we will not use the word "opinion" to describe matters of taste, although many people do. When someone expresses a like or dislike of a food or a fashion or a sport, you may often hear someone else say, "Well, that's just your *opinion*." Actually, it is a matter of taste.

How Does an Argument Develop?

It is appropriate to acknowledge and respect the fact that people are going to have different likes and dislikes in terms of tastes. We will refine our vocabulary: we will reserve the word opinion for considered views that have been developed with research and reasons. (See the discussion of opinions given by authorities in the section on evidence.) Our next task is to identify how such an opinion is developed.

We will not be using the word "right" at the end of our arguments. We might think that the person who wins an argument is "right." Not necessarily. A person who is clever at arguing can often get you to agree with him or her, even when you suspect he or she is wrong. A good lawyer can make a guilty person seem innocent. Furthermore, often when there are two sides to an issue, neither side is really "right" or "wrong". Some of the world's most challenging issues have good thinkers on both sides of the debate.

We can, however, judge the success of a debate. The point of argument or debate is to get the other person to agree with you and even to persuade the person to act as you would wish.

If you are effective at persuasion, you might get a friend to vote the way you would like, write a letter to a political representative or send money to your favorite cause. To achieve this success, to persuade effectively, you will want a clear answer to our second question, "How does an argument develop?" We will look at the argument process and identify the steps necessary for making a strong argument.

Developing an Argument

Arguments or debates generally follow this four-step format:

> **Step 1. We start by stating the point to be argued.** This point to be argued is called the "proposition," and we will study this concept here in Chapter 2.
>
> **Step 2. We gather evidence to support the position.**
>
> **Step 3. We gather evidence to understand the opposition.** We will learn more about gathering evidence and organizing our findings in Chapter 3.
>
> **Step 4. We reason to a conclusion.** Reasoning is the heart of critical thinking, the focus of this book. Chapters 4, 5, 6 and 7 deal with the reasoning process. Chapter 8 outlines one of the common ways that both students and career researchers use the skills that you will learn in this book: writing a completed researched persuasive paper.

In the academic realm, students often write research papers to learn the process of persuasion firsthand. Many professionals use this guided process. Lawyers use "argument" to convince the jury. Politicians "argue" to get funding for a special project or to get enough votes to pass a new law. Scientists use this process to support their laboratory work and to convince the scientific world that a new theory is correct.

What is your career path? As you work through your daily life as a parent and homeowner, will you work with medicine, politics or the law?

Perhaps you will be a stay-at-home parent, trying to convince your own children to make good choices.

Perhaps you might be a state representative, arguing for funding for better roads in your home state.

Perhaps you will be a scientist, trying to show the effects of climate change.

Clearly, people in every walk of life need to have a working understanding of the argument process.

It's time to explore the first step of the debate process, establishing an arguable proposition.

The Proposition

To begin an argument, we determine the point to be argued. This starting point can be called the "issue", the "premise" or the "proposition." We will use the term proposition to identify the focus of our argument. To get started, we will work on developing an arguable proposition, which is a statement of the point we want to prove.

This may seem counterintuitive. You may be thinking, shouldn't we allow the argument to develop? Won't we come to the conclusion that is the point to be proven? How can we make a statement without working our way up to it? This may sound like it will lead to success, but it is like getting on a train without having named the destination. Without a clearly identified destination, the traveler may get on the train going in the wrong direction.

You may already be familiar with this concept. In geometry proofs, we start with the point to be proven, and in science labs, we start with a theorem that we intend to prove through a planned experiment. The pattern of investigation is called the scientific method.

Proving a point in debate is much the same; we must identify our goal at the beginning of the process. This goal is called the proposition:

The proposition is a statement of the point to be argued.

A strong proposition has five distinct characteristics. Follow this explanation of the five characteristics and work through the examples and practices to be able to write the best proposition.

Proposition characteristic #1

A "good" proposition is not about matters of verifiable fact or matters of taste. (You can review these terms by rereading the beginning of this chapter.)

Example: Two friends may be deciding which film to see. One friend may say, "We have to go to the 3D version of this film; it is the best version." The other friend may say "No, the 3D effects ruin the film." We should remember that a preference for 3D is a matter of personal taste, not a matter for debate. A compromise may be reached, but not through logical debate. Rather, one of the two friends will agree to accommodate the other.

As expressed in Chapter 1, people also find themselves in debates about factual information. The assertion "This is the coldest day of the year!" might be countered with "No, it's not! It was much colder three weeks ago." This specious debate should not go on; it can easily be resolved by checking weather bureau statistics.

Proposition characteristic #2

The proposition is stated in a declarative sentence: it makes an assertion or urges a course of action.

Example: People often ask, "Should restaurants allow smoking in the eating area?" This question is open for discussion, but it is not a proposition. To make it a proposition, we need to create a declarative sentence:

"Smoking in public eating areas should be banned."

Or, if the arguer wants to take the other side:

"Smoking in public eating areas should be allowed."

In formal debate, the statement of the point to be argued is called "the question." It is also stated in a declarative sentence. This causes some confusion, but it will help to remember that the "question" is the point of the discussion. (See "Begging the Question" in Chapter 6 for more on the meaning of the word "question.")

Proposition characteristic #3

The proposition may not carry any biased words.

> Poor proposition: "The inadequate city parking facilities must be improved."

A civic debate about spending community monies on a new parking garage may be in order, but it should not start with this poor proposition. If the parking facilities are inadequate, no debate is necessary. However, it may be necessary to pull in data on the number of cars, the number of shoppers who drive into the city and whether a garage would be better than an open lot. These items would come into play to show whether or not the parking facilities are, in fact, inadequate.

To give the argument a fair start, the word "inadequate" should be removed. A good proposition would read like this:

> "Community funds should be earmarked for improving city parking facilities."

Note: For more information on using biased wording in arguments, see "Begging the Question" in Chapter 5.

Proposition characteristic #4

The proposition must be clear, not ambiguous.

Vocabulary Hint: The "ambi" in ambiguous means "both." If someone reads an ambiguous statement, they may see two possible ideas at the same time. It is important to write the sentence carefully so that we cannot imagine more than one possible meaning in the proposition.

We must edit an ambiguous statement so that it becomes a clear proposition.

To understand how to edit a proposition to remove ambiguity, work through this example:

> The headmaster of a school would like the school directors to provide funding for a summer program that will focus on skills that promote success in the workplace. The headmaster wants the program to be limited to those students who have already demonstrated strong scholastic success. The directors receive a proposal, "Students with B averages will be admitted to the summer program."

One school director asks, "If a student has an B average in just one class, will that student be eligible?'

Another director asks, "A student who has an A in biology, but only a C in calculus, has a B average. Will that student be eligible to attend the summer program?"

The school directors want the headmaster to defend his plan for the summer program. But before they begin, they need to know exactly which students are eligible to attend the program.

The original announcement is *ambiguous.* There are several ways to interpret it, and the wording should be clarified before debate on supporting the program can begin. When the headmaster is approached to clarify the qualifications for admission to the program, he thinks to himself, "What I really meant was that a student would have to have at least a B in each subject to be eligible." The headmaster realizes that he should reword his proposal to remove any ambiguity:

> Good proposition: "Students who have a B or better average in each of the subjects they are enrolled in this semester will be eligible to attend the summer program."

Now, everyone understands clearly what is being proposed, and the debate over funding the program can begin.

Proposition characteristic #5

The proposition must be singular. One cannot reasonably argue two ideas at once. Putting two ideas into one sentence does not mean they have become one idea. It is still not okay.

> Poor proposition: "Our employer should provide on-site day care for parents and improve exterior lighting."

While it is easy to see why employees might want to stack up several requests and present them to the employer all at once, clear thinking suggests that these two requests are quite different. In making his decision, the employer might agree to one and not the other. The most appropriate way to proceed is to separate the two issues and argue them separately.

To do this, you must write two separate propositions. Then, of course, you would have to proceed through the argument process with one at a time.

Better proposition #1: "Our company should provide on-site day care for working parents."

Better proposition #2: "Our company should improve exterior lighting."

A Note on Single Propositions and Politics: In the United States Congress, two or more different bills are often presented as one. A senator or representative might promote one idea, such as an increase on the tax on cigarettes, and a colleague might agree to vote for the bill if another request is attached to it, such as funding for a new reservoir in his home state. This addition is sometimes called a "rider" or an "earmark." The more picturesque term "pork" identifies the riders on a bill that are intended to bring federal dollars to a specific area or state. When the amount of government spending increases to meet the needs of these individual requests, we have "pork barrel spending." These disparaging descriptors remind us that arguing two things at one time, like voting for two ideas at the same time, is not the best way to proceed.

Practice Exercises on Propositions

Practice 2.a. Working with propositions

Directions:

> Step 1. Read each of the following sentences, and label each one GP for "good proposition" and NP for "not a good proposition."
>
> Step 2. For each NP, give the reason it is not acceptable using the five characteristics listed above.
>
> Step 3. Where possible, write each NP as a good proposition.

1. Toll highways should be eliminated throughout our country.
2. Modern art is too unusual to interest most people.
3. Schools should adopt a year-round school calendar and have all students wear uniforms.
4. Should the United Nations revisit the use of funds for UNICEF projects?
5. Sushi is just too exotic for the average restaurant patron.
6. Floyd Landis won the 2010 Tour de France.
7. Our company's inefficient delivery system should be revamped.

8. Vote for Tom Thompson for City Council.

9. The government should provide low interest loans to resolve the current housing crisis.

10. It is time for citizens to speak out against our city's irresponsible use of precious taxpayer dollars.

Practice 2.b. Research practice

Directions: Use a current source, such as a newspaper, news magazine or internet news source, to locate legislation that is currently up for vote in your area. Write the goal of the legislation as a simple proposition or explain why the legislation cannot be written as a proposition that fits the five characteristics of a good proposition.

Major and Minor Propositions

Now that you can create an arguable proposition, you should identify the minor propositions that will support your argument. These minor propositions will form the outline of your argument. Each minor proposition or issue should also follow the five characteristics of a strong proposition.

Vocabulary Note: The major and minor proposition are often called major and minor "premises." This word is used in the examples.

Here are three things to remember about minor premises:

1. A minor premise (or minor proposition) is a point that helps to show the sense of the major proposition. In the simplest terms, we see these as "reasons" to support our major proposition. Look at this example:

   Major premise: Capital punishment should be abolished.

   Minor premise: Capital punishment is not a deterrent to crime.

In this argument, the major goal is to prove that capital punishment is not acceptable. One reason the writer will give is that capital punishment does not stop people from committing this crime.

2. The minor premise itself may be debatable (as in the example above), in which case you have to argue (prove) it individually. People who are debating a major concern often call each minor premise an **issue.**

Vocabulary Note: Some debate formats call the major proposition "the issue."

You, the writer, are responsible for showing the relationship of the minor premise to the major premise.

Example:

> Many people are in favor of capital punishment because they believe it deters would-be murderers from committing their crime. The data shows that Country X, which has capital punishment, actually has a murder rate 12 percent higher than Country Y, which does not. Now that we have shown statistically that it does not appear to be a deterrent, hopefully people will abandon their support for capital punishment.

3. As you attempt to list supporting points to defend your main proposition, you should also be on the lookout for points that a person on the other side of the argument would use to prove his or her point. You will have to refute them in your paper.

Practice 2.c. Creating arguable propositions and identifying minor premises

Directions: For each question below, follow these steps:

Step 1. Form an arguable proposition.

Step 2. List at least three minor premises that would support the proposition.

Step 3. List two premises or reasons that the other side might use.

An example is provided.

Example: Should capital punishment be abolished?

Answer format:

Step 1. "The federal government should abolish capital punishment."

(The proposition must be rewritten as a declarative sentence.)

Step 2. Minor premises:

a. Capital punishment is not a deterrent to crime.

b. Capital punishment is discriminatory.

c. Capital punishment is revenge, not justice.

   d. Capital punishment is a poor use of tax dollars. (Capital punishment is more expensive than life imprisonment.)

Step 3. Reasons or premises the other side might raise:

   a. Capital punishment is the appropriate punishment for first-degree homicide.

   b. Capital punishment keeps known murderers from ever reoffending.

Follow the directions above, and use the example to guide you through these five questions.

1. Should elementary schools, schools for students under 10 years of age, eliminate all homework?

2. Should the first year at all state-supported colleges and universities be free?

3. Should the United Nations sponsor an international identification card?

4. Do we need a speed limit on major highways?

5. Should the 3-mile fishing limit be expanded?

In completing this exercise, you will demonstrate that you can begin an argument or debate with a strong proposition and organize your argument using minor premises. You are ready for the next step in preparing an argument: Gathering Evidence. After you complete the Chapter Review, move on to Chapter 3.

Chapter Review

1. It is inappropriate to argue about _____ or _____.

2. We enter into a debate to persuade people to change their minds about an issue, or more importantly, to get them to _____ on your idea.

3. List the four steps in developing an argument.

4. The statement of the question to be argued is called a _____.

5. A point that must be proven to support the major proposition is called a _____ or an _____.

6. List the five characteristics of a strong proposition.

7. These five propositions are flawed. Use the five characteristics of a strong proposition to explain why each one should be rewritten.

    - Should the International Olympic Committee lower the age of gymnasts to 14?

    - Music videos are too edgy for people over 45.

    - Here at The Snack Shoppe, we should be permitted to trade scheduled hours and also be given a $.10 per hour wage increase.

    - This spring has been the rainiest spring season in the last five years.

    - Our company's process of selecting mid-level supervisors is patently unfair.

8. Identify the only three items in Question 7 that have the potential to be strong propositions. Rewrite them in the correct form.

9. Web activity. Use any electronic news source to find a video of a debate between two candidates running for an elected position. The focus of such a debate is to show the strength of each candidate. As you watch the debate, identify the issues that are discussed.

10. List three or four important issues that are currently hot topics at your school or workplace. Select one and write it as an arguable proposition.

RESEARCH AND GATHERING EVIDENCE

The next step in formulating your argument is gathering evidence. Evidence is the collection of facts, statistics and professional opinions that are used to support a proposition.

Collecting evidence on your topic requires two steps:

1. **Gather** all available evidence using the library or online research.
2. **Evaluate** all the evidence that you find.

Gathering Evidence

It is important to gather all the evidence you possibly can to support your side of a debate. You need to look in all possible places; this is not the time to commit any "sins of omission." Forensics experts and crime detectives spend hours looking over every detail of a crime scene. Researchers in academia are required to review the "history of literature" in their field before publishing any new findings. And to argue responsibly, you should do the same: read and look, look and read, and then look more for all of the information available on your topic.

Your first efforts to gather evidence might be quite casual; you may see something in the daily newspaper, on a television news show or on the internet. If you see something that is potentially valuable, treat it appropriately: note the source, the date and other citation information.

More formal research evidence for arguments usually starts in the library or media center. Using the modern library efficiently is an important skill in researching. If you are unfamiliar with research techniques, especially with how to use the multitude of online sources, ask a librarian to help you.

Today's librarian is often called a "media specialist." That is because libraries now contain many types of research tools. Beyond the usual internet sites we find when surfing the web, the media specialist in any school or public library can direct you to reliable collections, databases, online journals and search engines to help you find all the evidence available on your topic.

Most schools and libraries have subscriptions to databases that offer strong, dependable information from peer-reviewed journals and other sources. Make use of these databases when you research and ask the librarian to guide you as you get started.

Gather evidence responsibly. Keep careful notes on the appropriate citation information needed for each source and give credit where credit is due. Keep the material you find. If you need instruction on the two most common citation formats, MLA (Modern Languages Association) and APA (American Psychological Association), you can again ask the media specialist. You can also find online tutorials on citations.

Treat sources and the environment with respect. Never tear an article out of a journal. Make as few copies as possible. If you locate a particularly long article in an online publication, plan carefully before you print to avoid waste. Use the highlight feature on the computer and select only the information you need before you press "print." Take care with the environment and print as little as possible. Save source material electronically whenever possible.

Practice good housekeeping when you research. More and more research involves printouts and copies, unlike the more conventional "note card" approach. If you highlight or underline, use a notation system in the margins of the copy to indicate different subtopics of the main idea. Many twenty-first century students have discarded the note card process, but it may be necessary if you are using items on reserve or in vertical files. Again, mark your note cards by subtopic to stay organized.

A common error is to look for quick and easily found supporting evidence to bolster an argument. Sometimes, this is purposeful: propagandists often list a quick series of facts that make their side look good. (See **stacking the deck** in the section on evaluating evidence.) A fair-minded researcher looks diligently for all the available evidence, including the information that supports the other side. Remember, in a serious debate, at some point you will have to refute information presented by the opposition. You may find the evidence for the other side is better; researchers often change their position and move to the other side of an argument when significant research supports the other side.

Evaluating Evidence

While you are researching, you must evaluate all the evidence you accumulate. We can evaluate information in several ways, determining whether the information is credible or not. The first consideration is where the information comes from, and in the twenty-first century, that often means the internet, so we will start there.

Online availability of information has changed the way both the average person and serious researchers look for information. As we set out to gather information, we must immediately think about evaluating the material we find on the web. How do we evaluate these sources?

The best way to start the evaluation process of online sources is to look at the "dot." Websites commonly end in one of these four "dots": .com, .org, .edu or .gov. These useful suffixes give us an important means of analyzing the site and the evidence it provides.

Four common network domains and their value in research

.com sites. These are the most common sites on the internet. The "com" means "commercial." These sites are set up and paid for by businesses and their commercial sponsors. Many of them are very good, and most site builders try to be fair and accurate. But it is important to remember that the site provider's basic concern is profit, not information. Another domain indicator, **.net**, (for "network") is used by networking sites and can appear as an alternate to .com.

.org sites. These sites are set up by organizations that have a specific agenda they want to promote. They may provide objective information and data, but often, they select data that promotes their cause. When we use such information, we should make it clear where it came from. Likewise, when we analyze an article or essay, we should notice when .org sites are used. This may be a clue that the material promotes one side of the argument.

Special interest groups often use .org sites to get information out on the web. Always go to another site to check data that comes from a .org site as special interest groups sometimes **stack the deck.** Also called **card stacking,** this is the practice of providing only facts that support a special cause, and carefully omitting facts that may not promote the cause. Although these facts are correct, they provide an inaccurate, one-sided view of the issue.

.edu sites. These sites are provided by educational groups, colleges and universities. They are one of the most reliable sources for information. Of course, even a college or university, especially if it is funded by a special group, might have its own agenda. Be a critical reader when you see the .edu marker.

.gov sites. These sites are provided by government agencies and generally provide the most reliable information. Go to a .gov site when you need demographic data on things like ages and populations, or any information that can be gathered on a government site, like weather, medical or crime statistics. Military sites, **.mil**, are similar to .gov sites, but are generally more restricted.

Select your sources carefully and responsibly when you research on the internet.

Whether you find your evidence on the web or in more conventional sources like books and periodicals, keep in mind these important considerations in evaluating all evidence:

To be valuable to your argument, your evidence must be either verifiable or provided by a reliable source. The following paragraphs provide helpful explanations of these two types of acceptable evidence.

Good evidence is **verifiable**. This means you can look it up in a dictionary, encyclopedia or textbook, or in the records kept by a concerned organization (the Weather Bureau, the NFL, the Dept. of Vital Statistics, etc.). "Reported" facts published in magazines and newspapers are only as reliable as the publishing company itself. This may help you understand why information found in the *Wall Street Journal* is generally more acceptable than that found in a celebrity magazine.

Good evidence can be attested to by a **reliable source or authority**. This, of course, is a little trickier. It's important to show that the source actually is reliable and knowledgeable. Only a well-known psychologist will be asked to comment on a defendant's mental health in a court trial. A world-renowned economist, not your neighbor, will be asked to comment about the economy on the evening news.

In a criminal case, investigators may have to take testimony from anyone on the scene of a crime. The "eyewitness" might be careful and observant, or have bad eyesight and hearing. The police have to take what they get. But in a serious debate, we have the responsibility to select strong authorities. In court, these authorities are called "expert witnesses." In debate, such an authority may also be called "an expert" or a "reliable source."

- An expert, or expert witness, may be asked to give information about a subject (just what is manic depression?) or his opinion (was the defendant clinically depressed at the time of the murder?).

- A reliable source must be physically and mentally capable and, of course, honest.

- An opinion given by an authority on a subject is often called an "educated guess."

Vocabulary Note: Serious journalists often cite a **reliable source** when they break a news story or cover a controversial event. Laws are in place to protect both the journalist's and the source's privilege of confidentiality. Magazines and newspapers that focus on celebrities often cite a **reliable source** as the point of information to share inside information about the lives of the stars.

In both situations – the frivolous and the serious – journalists protect their sources. But for educational purposes, in serious research and in debate, we always identify and provide a citation for our experts and reliable sources.

Using Peer-Reviewed Sources

The best way to know that you are looking for information in a reliable source is to make good use of **peer-reviewed** sources. These journals and article collections contain material that has been reviewed by recognized authorities in the given field before they are published. Your librarian will help you locate journals in all major fields of research that are professional and peer reviewed. Knowing that the information and data in the article has passed muster by a review board before the article was published will give you confidence that the information is reliable. Information in peer-reviewed sources is the most reliable information available in almost all subject areas.

Recognizing Bad Evidence

If all this seems fairly reasonable, you may wonder where "bad" evidence comes from. Unfortunately, there is a lot of bad, or flawed, evidence that is used to bolster poor arguments. If you recognize bad evidence, you can easily refute the argument of someone who uses it. Review these signs of unreliable evidence.

Old information is rarely useful

A poor arguer might says, "AIDS is not a problem here in our community. I have a pamphlet here that says there are no cases in our town or the surrounding areas." When you look at the poor arguer's data, you respond, "Your evidence is bad; that pamphlet was printed in 2001. Old evidence is not reliable. In fact, a 2009 news release from the department of health shows that there were 12 reported cases of AIDS in our community last year."

It is important to be current. Check the dates on your sources. A history book that only goes to 1976 is a poor choice for the twenty-first century. A cancer patient doesn't want to be treated with methods from the 1970s. And a twenty-first century research paper shouldn't use information from a 1977 almanac.

Facts can be reported incorrectly

Last week, two popular magazines talked about a popular movie star. One magazine said she has won five Academy Awards; the other said she has won one. They can't both be right. If you find discrepancies in information, keep searching. Look for the data that is reported most frequently, and by the most reliable source.

Facts can be stated correctly, but in a misleading way

Two patients are wondering which hospital has the highest success rate in treating their illness. One patient says, "I am going to Hospital A, because over half of their patients get well, whereas fewer than half of the patients at Hospital B get better."

How would you feel if you found out that the gentleman meant 49 percent when he said "Fewer than half" and 51 percent when he said "More than half"? In this case, the arguer knew that the data did not reveal a significant difference, so he used language in a clever way to make the "data" fit his argument.

This example reminds us of the power of language. A strong argument often uses data and statistics to make a point, but language can muddle the issue. Read and listen carefully as you gather your data.

And, while this textbook focuses on the logic of language, this is a good time to remind everyone: always do the math.

Try this fun example to see what happens when we play with numbers:

> Only 2 out every 100 children will eat broccoli. If you sprinkle the broccoli with cheese, the number of children who will eat it increases by 50 percent.
>
> How many children out of 100 will eat broccoli sprinkled with cheese?

Take a moment with a pencil and paper to compute your answer. Did you get the answer "three children" or a lot more? Three is the correct answer. Look at this more serious example, and then we'll review how to do the math:

> Recently, some doctors noted that hormone therapy caused a "50 percent increase" in certain types of cancer in women. The general

public was alarmed – a 50 percent increase sounds like a lot. But what does that really mean?

Here is the math:

Three out of every 1,000 women between the ages of 25 and 50 can expect to be diagnosed with breast cancer. If this number "increases" by 50 percent, what does that mean? How do we find out? We multiply 3 × .50, and then add it to 3 to find the new number of women diagnosed with the illness.

$$(3 \times .50) + 3 = 4.5$$

Now we can see that hormone therapy will result in 4.5 women becoming ill. That is out of 1,000 women. At this point, this does not seem like such a huge increase. The phrase "50 percent increase" takes on a different meaning when we do the math. It is an increase, but it is not as frightening. And, as the health services recommend, the best decision on whether to take these drugs comes from one's own physician.

We all know the old saying, "Figures don't lie, but a lot of liars figure." Even when it is unintentional, people toss data around to sound knowledgeable. To win an argument, some will use selected data to create fear. Always check on data and use your basic math skills to review the numbers.

"Doing the math" is one way that helps arguers see the sense of an idea.

Some folks like to say, "I don't do math in public," but you should always be prepared to work through the calculations of data that you find in your research.

The "voice of authority" must be used wisely

Sometimes we rely on statements made by knowledgeable people to provide evidence or understanding. However, it is important to note that authority by success, authority by transference and the "testimonial" are not good uses of authority.

Just because a celebrity is a "star," this doesn't mean he is an authority on life insurance (authority by success.) Don't ask your doctor how to invest your money (authority by transference.) And it shouldn't matter to the consumer that a popular singer uses a particular make-up (testimonial).

Recognizing bad evidence may help you spot a bad argument when you hear one. It will help you become a more critical television viewer and a more intelligent consumer.

The Next Step: Organizing Evidence

As you collect your evidence, you should organize and double-check as part of the process. Here's how:

1. **Organize** by "minor premises." In Chapter 2, we learned how to start our debate by setting up our major proposition, which is the main point to be argued. Then we learned to identify the parts of the argument, the "minor premises." Use these minor premises to create a basic outline, with one minor premise for each outline section. Do as much of this work as you can before you start your research. Then, as you locate evidence, place the "information bites" into the outline in the correct section.

2. **Triangulate** to check your information. This means that you look for important pieces of information in three different sources. If you find the same numbers or facts in two places, you can be fairly well satisfied. But if you discover an inconsistency, you must move to a third source to check for accuracy.

Additional points about the search for information:

The news media is not obligated by law to use good evidence, to get its facts straight or to report all of the news that comes into its central office. Negative press is often good press for an actor or actress, and frequently, scandalous-sounding tabloid headlines about famous people are so outlandish that they refuse to acknowledge them.

The news media often cites a "reliable source." In the world of journalism, this concept has a lot more leeway. Unlike the "expert witness" in a criminal case, the journalist's reliable source may not be a true expert and the reader may not even know who the reliable source is. We must be careful, critical readers of news stories.

When an authority speaks, you must consider if he or she has anything to gain. If so, his or her statements (opinions) may be suspect. Expert witnesses in court cases are often paid, and there are judicial rules about the selection of such a witness and the payment. Always look for this additional information when you hear the opinions of an "expert."

Consider you audience. Advertisers do – that's why they pick popular athletes to advertise sports gear and mature celebrities to advertise insurance to retired people.

Practice Exercises in Gathering Evidence

Use this list of topic choices to complete the research practices. You can use the internet to complete the practice, but it is recommended that you use a computer in your school library. Ask the librarian for help if you run into a challenge. Remember, the modern librarian – also called the media specialist – knows how to do more than find books. Connect with the library specialist to get the help you need and learn to use the most advanced research tools, including the databases to which your school subscribes.

Topic choices: Airline safety/pilot training

Current influenza epidemics

Teen pregnancy

Practice 3.a. Finding facts and reliable opinions

Select one current topic from the list above or from a project list you have been given at school or at work. Then go to the library or go online and find five verifiable facts and four opinions from reliable authorities about the topic.

Practice 3.b. Refining the "dot" search

Using the "dot" sites on the internet, research the same topic you focused on in 3.a. Find two "information bites" from each of the four common sites: .com, .org, .edu and .gov.

Practice 3.c. Peer review search

Ask the librarian or media specialist to help you locate two or more peer-reviewed journals that have articles on your subject. Read an article or two on your subject. On your first, preliminary read-through of an article, take note of the professional tone and requirements for citations. Then, read the article again to highlight information you would use for a research project.

Practice 3.d. Coordinating research with major and minor premises

To complete this practice, you will research the topic "capital punishment." Using the five minor premises given in Chapter 2 for the topic "capital punishment," create a simple outline. Each section of your outline will be headed by one of the minor premises. Then, as you find information in your search, organize the information (evidence) by placing the facts/data/opinions in the correct section of the outline.

Practice 3.e. "Delving" for a thorough search

Review your capital punishment outline. If any section does not have three pieces of evidence, search again so that you have located three items for each section. Also, double check all data by locating it in a second source and triangulate to a third source if necessary.

Chapter Review

1. List the qualities of "good" evidence.
2. Identify the characteristics of "bad" evidence.
3. Define the following terms: "reliable authority," "reliable source" and "expert witness."
4. Compare the concept of a "reliable source" who might be asked a question in a court trial and a "reliable source" who might be mentioned by a journalist.
5. Presenting only the data that supports an arguer's preferred side of a debate is called _____.
6. Explain each of the popular "dot" sites.
7. Working with the capital punishment topic that we started in Chapter 2, find one source for this topic that is a .org site in favor of capital punishment and one .org site that is against it.
8. _____ means to check a data fact in three different sources.
9. Ask your librarian/media specialist to show you how to use search limiters. Then, practice this with the capital punishment topic and look for only those sources that are less than five years old.
10. We can organize the data we have found by grouping information in an outline that uses _____ as outline sections.

INDUCTIVE REASONING

Reasoning is the process by which we move from curiosity to a conclusion.

In the physical and social sciences, and in detective work, reasoning is the mental move from data (numbers, facts and evidence) to a supportable theory, which is more than just a guess.

Reasoning is possible because we recognize some regularity or order to the world around us.

Reasoning is a natural process of the human mind; all people of normal intelligence can reason to some extent without being "taught" how. But like any skill, it can be developed further through study and practice.

The reasoning process is generally divided into two categories: **inductive reasoning** and **deductive reasoning**. In this chapter, we will discuss induction, the most natural and common form of logic.

Generalization

Induction is the process of **generalization**. This process starts when we see that a number of instances are the same, or that a pattern repeats itself. Then, we make a mental statement that affirms the pattern. If our new next-door neighbor greets us with a smile today, and says hello with a smile the next few times we see him, we think, "Oh, he is a friendly person."

Scientific theory works by the process of generalization. For example, after a long period of observation, scientists noted that water freezes at 0°C. Then, a statement was made about that observation: "Water freezes at 0°C." We call these statements "laws" or "rules," but actually, they are generalizations.

The same is true for the "rules" of grammar in each language. One might think that there is a grammar guru out there, making all the rules before people start to speak. In fact, the "rules" of grammar are just observations about the way most people use the language most of the time.

We make generalizations in our everyday activities. If coffee, milk and meat are less expensive at the Super Shop, the shopper will say, "I always go to Super Shop…things are cheaper there."

There may be exceptions: not everything will be cheaper at the Super Shop, and water doesn't always freeze at 0°C, but our minds still make the mental move from "some" to "all." This is called the **inductive leap**.

How do we know if we can trust a generalization? A set of guidelines does exist. Induction (generalization) is a reliable method of reasoning as long as the following criteria are met.

Tests for generalization

1. A fair number of instances must be investigated. (Basing a generalization on too few instances is a major error in reasoning. This error is called **"hasty generalization"** or **"jumping to conclusions."**)

2. Instances must be typical.

3. Negative instances must be explained.

Practice 4.a. Apply the three tests for generalization to the following practices

1. I've been to visit my Aunt Ida's home in Manchester twice and the weather was perfect both times. It would be great to live in Manchester, where the weather is always great.

2. I was worried about moving to a small town, because the small town where my sister lives seems to experience a lot of crime. Then I saw a recent study of 20 small towns in our region. The number of crimes was compared to nearby cities, and the crime in the small towns was noticeably less. I think that generally, small towns are safer than cities.

3. Maryellen was afraid to take amoxicillin because her friend Amy had an allergic reaction to it. Maryellen's doctor told her to read the prescription information, where she would see that allergic reactions occur in less than one out of every 100 users.

The Analogy

A second type of inductive reasoning is reasoning by **analogy**. It is based on the concept that if two things are alike in a number of important points, they will be alike in the point in question.

An analogy is a comparison. Our mind tells us that by comparing something new to something familiar, we can make a conclusion about the new idea.

Here is an example: Jim asks his friend Joe, who is a great tennis player, to join him in a game of racquetball. Joe says, "I've never played racquetball." Jim says, "No problem. Racquetball is a racket sport, just like tennis. It takes stamina, speed, agility and the ability to hit the ball with a racquet. You have those qualities; you'll do fine."

Jim has reasoned that Joe will be good at racquetball because he is good at tennis. The sports are similar; this is good reasoning.

Reasoning by analogy works when two criteria are met:

1. The two instances compared are alike in important respects. (It would be foolish to argue that, because Jim is good at tennis, he'll be good at Trivial Pursuit.)

2. Differences can be accounted for as being unimportant. (In comparing tennis and racquetball, it hardly matters that one is played indoors and one outdoors.)

People use analogies every day, but they don't always know how to test them for validity. Consider this example:

Tina asks her parents, "Can I go to the school dance on Friday? Everyone is going." Her father responds, "Oh, everyone is going? I suppose if everyone jumped off a ten-storey building, you would want to do that too?" This is an age-old gambit of parents, but it actually doesn't hold up under scrutiny.

Why? Let's examine the analogy.

Going to a dance is nothing like jumping off a ten-storey building. The statement fails analogy criterion #1. These two instances *are not alike* in important respects. One is a chaperoned, school-sanctioned activity; the other is just foolish behavior.

Next, criterion #2: the differences are not unimportant. The difference is safety: a school dance is generally a safe place to be; jumping off a building is obviously dangerous.

Of course, Tina's father has the final say. But let's hope he has a good reason if he says no to Tina's request.

Now that you get the idea, you can practice with these analogies. Keep the two criteria in mind when you hear an analogy used as an argument.

Practice in Analogies

Practice 4.b.

In Chapter 1, the "Warm-up" section says, "Throughout the chapters of this text, readers will be exercising an important part of the body: the brain. Let's do what the athletes do: warm up." There is an implied analogy here – that the brain is like a muscle, and it can improve with exercise. Use the criteria for analogy listed above to evaluate this analogy.

Practice 4.c.

Mr Lahr's neighbor just put in an expensive home security system. Mr Lahr asked him if he thought the security system was worth the cost. "It's like our country's military defense system," the neighbor replied. "I'd rather not spend the money, and I hope I never need it, but there have been break-ins in other areas not too far from here. I'm away on business a lot. Just like the country needs a standing defense system, my home has to be protected. It would be irresponsible not to spend the money on it." Mr Lahr didn't want to spend the money on a home security system, but now that he has heard this analogy, he is thinking about it. Help Mr Lahr decide if this is a good analogy.

Practice 4.d.

Countries are often given "ages" that are analogous to the developmental stages of people. The United States is often described as being an "adolescent" in the world of nations. Identify the characteristics of adolescents and determine if this is a good analogy.

Analogy, Metaphor and Simile

When literature students read about analogies, they often ask, "Is an analogy the same as a metaphor or a simile?"

It is true that analogies, metaphors and similes are all types of comparison. Most students learn the distinction between similes and metaphors in the early grades. The key is that a simile starts with the words "like" or "as."

Now we have added the analogy. We know how these three devices are the same – they are all comparisons. But how are they different?

The difference lies in the purpose.

Similes and metaphors are literary techniques, also called figurative language. Author use this figurative language purposefully to enhance meaning.

Analogy is a reasoning process. The writer suggests a comparison between a new idea and a more familiar idea, with the express purpose of guiding the audience to a reasonable conclusion about the new idea.

More on induction

Remember the famous song from the musical *Annie*?

> *The sun will come out, tomorrow!*
>
> *Bet your bottom dollar, there'll be sun!*

Little orphan Annie was being more than just optimistic – she was using her head! We don't think about it much, but we depend on it: the sun will come out tomorrow; this has been happening for quite some time. Now that you know more about induction, you will see it in everyday life. Just remember to use the "tests" when you hear a generalization or an analogy.

Before we move on to deduction, review what you have learned about induction in the Chapter Review.

Chapter Review

1. Induction is the more formal word for _____.

2. The mental move from "some" to "all" is called the _____.

3. Making a generalization with too few samples is called _____ or _____.

4. The three tests for generalization/induction are

    a. _____

    b. _____

    c. _____.

5. Reasoning by comparison is known as making an _____.

6. The two criteria for making a good analogy are

   a. _____

   b. _____.

7. Similes and metaphors are used to _____.

   Analogies are used to _____.

5

DEDUCTIVE REASONING

Sherlock Holmes with his magnifying glass, the detective on the modern crime show using DNA – we all enjoy watching great sleuths solve crimes. What is their secret? They are all masters of deduction.

In deductive reasoning, we move from an accepted generalization to a particular application of that general notion.

For example, you know that St Bernard dogs are quite large. This is a generalization (or "rule"): "St Bernard dogs are large." If you get a St Bernard puppy, it's fair to assume that *this* puppy (the particular application) will be quite large when it grows up.

Just like we do with induction, we use deductive reasoning in ordinary, everyday situations. We also use our deductive powers when we read mystery novels and try to solve the case along with the detective. Police investigators use this process too.

Thinking by Classifying: Venn Diagrams

Deduction is also called "reasoning by classes." The human mind will put like with like, forming groups, categories or classes of information. We can improve our deductive skills by honing our classification skills. Then, we make deductions based on these classes/categories.

Let's start by reviewing our categorizing skills. One way to make this easier is to use a diagram called a Venn diagram.

Here are two examples, followed by a set of ten that you can use to practice:

Example 1: A cow is a mammal.

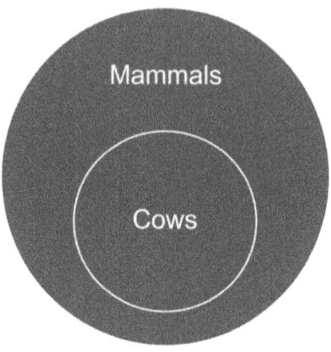

Example 2: The silver maple is a deciduous tree.

For Example 2, two diagrams are provided. The diagram with three circles adds a category (trees) that is implicit in the statement. This "implicit" category can be helpful in getting started.

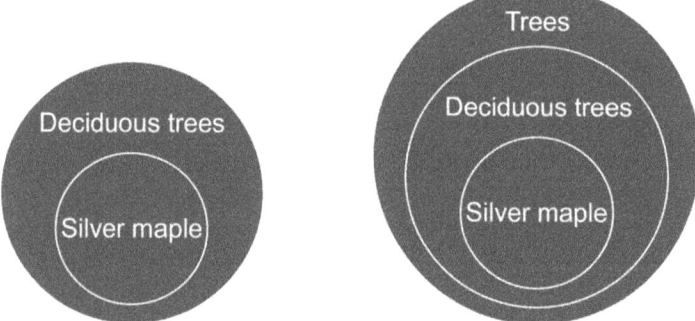

As you can see by the diagrams, the idea is to show which category is larger and contains the smaller category. This may seem simple, but as you work through the practice, you may discover that you are sometimes challenged to see which category is larger.

5.a. Practice in classification

Directions: Create a Venn diagram for each example. Check your work with a partner first. Then go to the answers section in the back of this text to check your work.

1. The Big Dipper is a constellation.
2. Zebras are striped animals.
3. All members of the baseball team are boys.
4. Only citizens can vote.
5. Brie is a cheese.
6. Milk is a healthy drink.
7. Even kings die.
8. None but the brave deserve the fair.
9. Only the brave deserve the fair.
10. Good men are devoted to their families.

Items eight, nine and ten test another important skill: **precision in language use**. The phrases "only" and the more sophisticated "none but the" will challenge you to determine which group is larger. Item ten challenges our mindset. In item one, you probably found it easy to identify "constellation" as the big group and the Big Dipper as an item inside the bigger circle. For item ten, you will have to think twice about which circle will be bigger on your Venn diagram. Check the answers in the back of the book for further explanation. Understanding these more complex ideas will be important when we use our deductive skills to reason about abstract ideas.

A special note about "some": Venn diagrams also show when two classes overlap. Take, for example, the categories "metals" and "conductors." Our statement might be "Some metals are conductors." The Venn diagram would look like this:

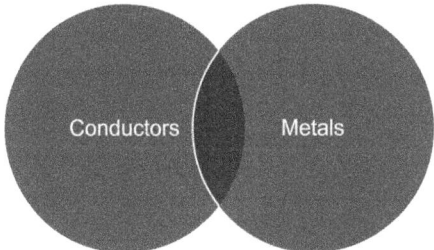

However, in deductive reasoning, we are hoping to come to a definite conclusion, not a "sometimes" conclusion. To that end, this text will work only with categories that fit completely within bigger categories. If you are interested in working through additional ideas regarding classification, you may want to take an advanced course in logic and critical thinking after you have mastered the basics in this textbook.

Reasoning by Classification: The Syllogism

In the process of deduction, we come to a "conclusion" by setting up classes, or groups, and then using the grouping process to make a determination about a particular item.

We can use Venn diagrams to demonstrate this process, and then we can move on to processing the ideas verbally in a logic pattern called the **syllogism**. Here is an example using the St Bernard dogs that we introduced at the beginning of the chapter.

Example: In general conversation, we mention that Joe has a St Bernard. We haven't seen this dog yet, but we know that "all St Bernards are large," so it is easy to make a "deduction" about Joe's new dog: it will be large.

If we make a Venn diagram, it will look like this, to start:

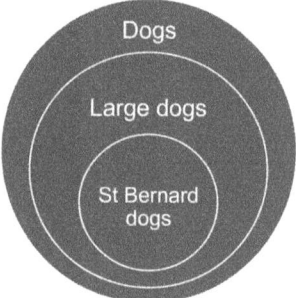

When we think about a particular application (Joe's dog), we put the words outside of the Venn diagram and draw an arrow into it, showing where Joe's dog fits. Since we know that the new dog is a St Bernard, we draw the arrow in to St Bernards, and we "see" that this dog is in the "large dog" category. The diagram helps us visualize the groupings, and visualization helps us come to a sensible conclusion.

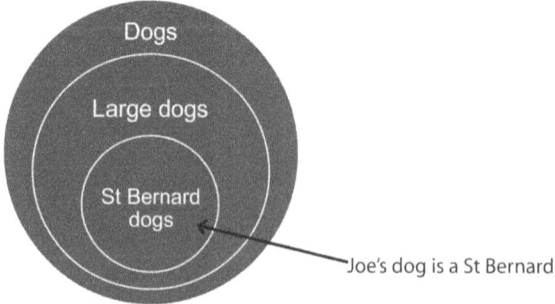

Sometimes visualization of categories is challenging, especially when we are dealing with abstract ideas. We use diagrams and visualization to get us started, but because our challenge in this textbook is working with language and logic, we want to develop the skill of working with words, not pictures.

In the study of logic, we want to complete the deductive process with language. So, we duplicate this same thought process by using a **three-step language pattern** called the **syllogism.** The steps look like this:

Syllogism Example:

> All purebred St Bernard dogs are large.
>
> Joe's dog is a St Bernard.
>
> Therefore, Joe's dog is large.

To eliminate the repetition of the word "therefore," logicians replace it with the symbol "∴" at the beginning of the third line of the syllogism. We will follow the logician's pattern and use the ∴ as we proceed with practice in syllogisms.

Using Venn Diagrams to Understand the Syllogism

The Venn diagram complements and can be used as a test for the syllogism. Because it is easier to "see" the process, we will start with Venn diagrams to practice our skills of deduction.

Use the Venn diagram to determine which group is part of another. Identifying the larger group and then the subgroup will help you think in classes. This is a good way to begin the process of deductive reasoning.

Here are some examples of syllogisms paired with three-step Venn diagrams:

Example 1:

> All zebras have black and white stripes.
>
> That animal is a zebra.
>
> ∴ That animal has black and white stripes.

Make a Venn diagram that shows that this is good reasoning. After you work with Example 2, compare both of your diagrams with the diagrams and explanation below.

Example 2:

The ermine changes color to match the season.

That animal changes color to match the season.

∴ That animal is an ermine.

Make a Venn diagram for Example 2. Does your diagram show that this is good reasoning, or does it reveal a flaw in the reasoning? Compare your diagram with the sample below.

Example 1, diagram:

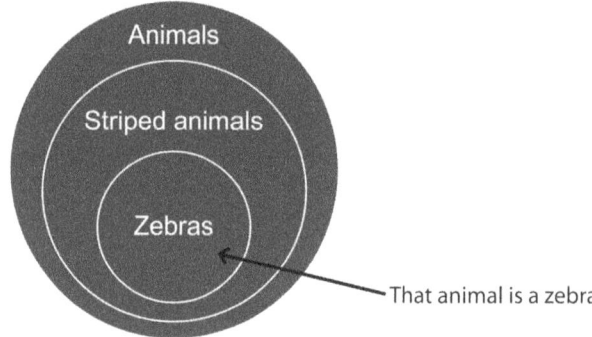

You are probably thinking, "Yes, this makes sense." It is easy to see that if that animal is a zebra, it is also in the "Animals with Black and White Stripes" circle. This syllogism is **valid**.

Now, look at **Example 2, diagram**:

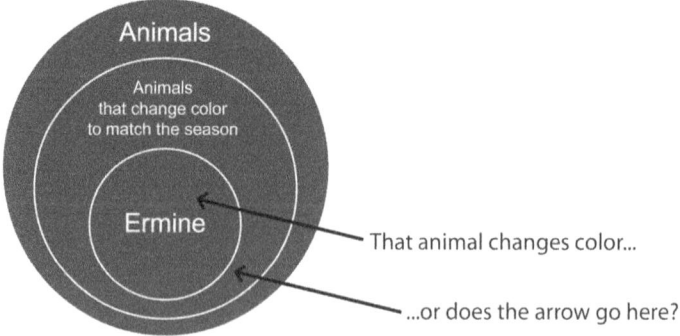

In this diagram, we know we should draw the arrow into the middle circle, indicating that "that animal changes color." But there are no words to indicate

DEDUCTIVE REASONING

that the arrow should go all the way into the third, inner circle that indicates the ermine. We end up with a question mark: We don't know for sure. This syllogism is **invalid**.

Now we are ready to move from Venn diagrams to syllogisms. Practice 5.b will give you the skills necessary to move from mental pictures of grouping to thinking about grouping and deduction in syllogisms.

Practice 5.b. Using Venn diagrams to check syllogisms

Directions: Use the examples above to guide you. Make Venn diagrams for these practice items to test the validity of each syllogism. After you make the diagram, indicate **valid** ("good reasoning") or **invalid** ("bad reasoning") after each one.

1. Cats are mammals.

   The Siamese is a cat.

   ∴ The Siamese is a mammal.

2. Metals expand when heated.

   Steel is a metal.

   ∴ Steel expands when heated.

3. The evening news begins at 6:00 p.m.

   The show she's watching started at 6:00 p.m.

   ∴ She's watching the evening news.

4. Dictionaries contain definitions of words.

   This book is a dictionary.

   ∴ This book contains definitions of words.

5. All zebras have ears.

   People have ears.

   ∴ People are zebras.

6. A professional photographer takes pictures.

   Mark takes pictures.

   ∴ Mark is a professional photographer.

7. The American Thanksgiving holiday always falls on the fourth Thursday in November.

   This year, 22 November is the fourth Thursday in November.

   ∴ This year, 22 November is Thanksgiving.

8. All four-legged animals are quadrupeds.

   Cows have four legs.

   ∴ All cows are quadrupeds.

9. All ninth graders must pass English to move to the tenth grade.

   Vicki is a ninth grader

   ∴ Vicki must pass English to move to the tenth grade.

10. Bran is a cereal.

    Mindy eats cereal for breakfast.

    ∴ Mindy eats bran for breakfast.

Check your responses with the answers in the appendix of this text. Work through the explanations for the more challenging syllogisms. At this point, you are ready to see how we use syllogistic reasoning to make deductions.

How is syllogistic reasoning used in real life? Imagine this everyday conversation:

> Gerry says, "I think that young man attends an expensive private school."
>
> "Why?" asks Jim.
>
> "Because he has on a white shirt and a tie, and I know that the students in expensive private schools have to wear shirts and ties."

Now, people make observations like this all of the time. But if you put it into syllogistic form, you may suspect that it is not correct.

> All students attending expensive private schools wear white shirts and ties.
>
> That young man is wearing a white shirt and tie.
>
> ∴ That young man attends an expensive private school.

If you are still not sure that this is invalid, make a Venn diagram to check the thinking. While your common sense may tell you that a young person might be wearing a white shirt and tie for many reasons, the diagram helps us see the big picture. You may also be getting glimpses of when the syllogism pattern doesn't work. Our ultimate goal is to evaluate syllogisms without the Venn diagram.

The three-part syllogism can be hidden in natural, everyday language. We see this in the field of law, which relies on deductive reasoning. Lawyers present syllogistic proof to the jury, but they generally present the syllogistic process in a conversational tone that may partially conceal the pattern. Our minds pick up on this pattern subconsciously. It helps to reset the ideas in their three-part mode so that we can examine their validity.

Look at this example, in which a lawyer tries to demonstrate his client's good character to get the jury's sympathy:

> "Ladies and Gentlemen of the Jury, we all know that good men are devoted to their families, and Mr Lyons is devoted to his family. Clearly, Mr Lyons is a good man."

Use a Venn diagram to determine if this is good or bad reasoning. Your biggest problem will be deciding which category is the larger category, "good men" or "men who are devoted to their families." You can refer to item ten in Practice 5.a to help you with your deductive skills. When you draw a Venn diagram and check your answer, you may be surprised to find that "men devoted to their families" is the larger category. Mr Lyons may not, contrary to the lawyer's assertion, fit into the smaller, "good men" category.

Review the answers in the back of the book and you will begin to understand how the legal profession uses logic. Try one more for fun:

> The crime was committed by a left-handed person.
>
> My client is not left-handed.
>
> ∴ My client could not have committed the crime.

Since "my client" cannot even be placed in the circle of left-handed people, we can see that the client is clearly out of the inner circle, the criminal. The client is exonerated.

Detectives use deduction all of the time. The evidence they collect at the scene of the crime often becomes the larger circle. The application of evidence to the suspect becomes the inner circle. Then the detectives, the lawyers and ultimately the jury, make the mental move to the "therefore" line – either guilt or innocence – in the syllogism.

Working with the Syllogism without Diagrams

As you have seen in the Venn diagram practice, the syllogism is a three-part formal argument. The syllogism follows a formal pattern, and we can test syllogisms with our visual skills. Working at a higher skill level, we can learn to test the validity of a syllogism without making a Venn diagrams.

To do this, we need to use the "vocabulary" of syllogisms. Four key terms are:

1. **Major premise**
2. **Minor premise**
3. **Conclusion**
4. **Validity**, including the terms **valid** and **invalid**

The first line states the generalization that begins the argument; it is called the **major premise**.

The second premise states the particular situation to which the major premise is applied; it is called the **minor premise**.

The third line starts with the symbol ∴ which we read as "therefore." This third line reveals the deductive move to the **conclusion**.

You can learn to apply these three terms by looking at an easy example:

All red apples are ripe. (**Major premise**)

This apple is red. (**Minor premise**)

∴ This apple is ripe. (**Conclusion**)

This syllogism is **valid** – not because it is true, but because it is systematically argued. It follows the format of the syllogism: "All X is Y. This ★ is an X. Therefore, this ★ must be a Y."

Remember, *valid* does not mean true; it means correctly argued.

Look at this example:

> All ripe apples are red.
>
> This apple is ripe.
>
> ∴ This apple must be red.

This conclusion is **valid**, but obviously, it is not true. Some apples, like Granny Smiths, are green or yellow when they are ripe.

Thus, a primary rule of argument is that, in order to argue to a correct conclusion, you must start with a true premise. Now, some people will say that no sensible logician would accept an argument with false premises as valid.

That sounds simple and obvious. However, when you look at this next syllogism, you will see how we can encounter difficulties with deduction when we are working with abstract ideas.

Example:

> Spending government money on unworkable projects is foolish.
>
> The new climate change program is an unworkable project.
>
> ∴ Spending money on the new climate change program is foolish.

Is this good or bad reasoning? It is perfectly good reasoning. The conclusion is valid. But the question arises, is the new climate change program unworkable? The second premise states boldly that it is. This "logical deduction" is based on a strong statement that may or may not be true.

We might think that it is the responsibility of the arguer to prove his premises. However, it is also the responsibility of the opposition to demand that proof. Strong arguers do not blindly accepting bold statements. This takes us back to our evaluation of evidence in Chapter 3. If an idea is stated as "a fact," then it should be verifiable. We can look it up and find out for sure.

Can we test for **validity**? Yes. If the syllogism is made with true premises, there are ways to check if the reasoning has been done in a logical way. We are ready to explore the "checks" that show whether the process of deduction is **applied** in a valid or invalid way.

Several standard rules determine whether or not a syllogism is correctly processed. We will look at two pairs of those rules.

In order to understand the rules, we need to know four additional vocabulary words as they are used in syllogistic argument:

1. **Condition:** the first "half" of the major premise, i.e., the first concept or item in the first line of the syllogism. Grammatically, this is the subject of the first sentence.

2. **Consequence:** the second "half" of the major premise, i.e., the second concept or item in the first line of the syllogism. It is the predicate portion of the first sentence.

3. **Affirm:** The second line of the syllogism says that the condition or consequence does happen or does exist.

4. **Deny:** A "no" or "not" is added in the second line to suggest that the condition or consequence does not happen or does not exist.

For example, if the first line of the syllogism is "All cows eat grass," then

"All cows" is the **condition**,

and "eat grass" is the **consequence**.

Next, we work with the second line of the syllogism.

If the second line reads, "That animal *is a cow*," we have **affirmed the condition**.

If the second line reads, "That animal *eats grass*," we have **affirmed the consequence**.

If the second line reads, "That animal *is not a cow*," we have **denied the condition**.

If the second line reads, "That animal *does not eat grass*," we have **denied the consequence**.

Let's try to move through two syllogisms built on the "all cows" start. In the first two examples, we will work with the "affirming" process.

Example 1:

All cows eat grass.

That animal is a cow. (The condition "cows" is affirmed.)

∴ That animal eats grass.

You are probably thinking, "That makes sense!" What happens if we affirm the consequence?

Example 2:

All cows eat grass.

That animal eats grass. (The consequence "eats grass" has been affirmed.)

∴ That animal is a cow. (Does this seem right?)

Clearly, that is not correct. Your common sense tells you that "that animal" could be a horse, a goat, a sheep or any other animal that eats grass.

Now we know two of the rules that apply to processing syllogisms:

Rule 1: You can affirm the condition. The result will be **valid**.

Rule 2: You should not affirm the consequence. The result will be **invalid**.

Let's try two more "all cows" examples. In these next examples, we will work with the "deny" concept.

Example 3:

All cows eat grass.

That animal is not a cow. (The condition, "cow" has been denied.)

∴ That animal does not eat grass. (Does this seem right?)

You are probably thinking that this conclusion is invalid, and you are correct. Again, your common sense tells you that "that animal" could be one of the other animals that eat grass.

Example 4:

All cows eat grass.

That animal does not eat grass. (The consequence "eats grass" has been denied.)

∴ That animal is not a cow.

Again, your common sense comes in to play. If the animal does not eat grass, it can't possibly be a cow. Denying the consequence led us to a valid conclusion

Now we know two more rules about processing syllogisms:

> **Rule 3: You should not deny the condition.** The result will be **invalid**.
>
> **Rule 4: You can deny the consequence.** The result will be **valid**.

Four more examples should put us on firm footing with the process of deduction in these syllogisms. Work through these four examples to reinforce your understanding:

> Everyone caught speeding will be fined.
> George was caught speeding.   >>> You **can affirm** the condition.
> ∴ George will be fined.   Conclusion is **valid**.
>
> Everyone caught speeding will be fined.
> George was fined.   >>> You **should not affirm** the consequence.
> ∴ George was caught speeding.   Conclusion is **invalid**.
>
> All types of maple are deciduous.
> That tree is not deciduous.   >>> You **can deny** the consequence.
> ∴ That tree in not a maple.   Conclusion is **valid**.
>
> All types of maple are deciduous.
> That tree is not a maple.   >>> You **should not** deny the condition.
> ∴ That tree is not deciduous.   Conclusion is **invalid**.

Let's review our four working rules for checking the validity of syllogisms:

> **Rule 1: You can affirm the condition.** The result will be **valid**.
>
> **Rule 2: You should not affirm the consequence.** The result will be **invalid**.
>
> **Rule 3: You should not deny the condition.** The result will be **invalid**.
>
> **Rule 4: You can deny the consequence.** The result will be **valid**.

Two Important Notes:

1. We will work with these four rules. There are other rules that govern the processing of syllogisms beyond the basic "affirm" and "deny" rules. Perhaps you will study them in an advanced logic course. As a novice logician, work with these four rules.
2. Remember, these rules do not apply to syllogisms with "some."

Practice 5.c. Determining validity in syllogisms

Directions: Use the four rules above to determine the validity of each syllogism. Identify the rule (from the list of four rules above) that supports your answer. Remember that "valid" does not mean "true." If you want to comment on the "truth" of a conclusion, make an additional note on your answer sheet.

1. All students who go to Ludley School wear blue uniforms.

   That student is wearing a blue uniform.

   ∴ That student is from Ludley School.

2. Anyone who can't learn from experience is a fool.

   John can't learn from experience.

   ∴ John is a fool.

3. Birds migrate when the seasons change.

   Eskimos migrate when the seasons change.

   ∴ Eskimos are birds.

4. Communists believe in socialized medicine.

   Mr Brown believes in socialized medicine.

   ∴ Mr Brown is a communist.

5. All Labrador retrievers are black.

   The Smiths' new puppy is a Lab.

   ∴ The Smiths' new puppy is black.

   * If you are struggling with #5, review the directions at the beginning of this exercise. Remember, "valid' does not mean "true."

6. Those who are expelled are a disgrace to our school.

   George was not expelled.

   ∴ George is not a disgrace to our school.

7. The killer was in Detroit on the night of the murder.

   Spike was in Detroit on the night of the murder.

   ∴ Spike is the killer.

8. The killer was in Detroit on the night of the murder.

   Mugsey was not in Detroit on the night of the murder.

   ∴ Mugsey is not the killer.

9. The Department Chair must have a PhD.

   Mr Everett does not have a PhD.

   ∴ Mr Everett is not the Department Chair.

10. The winner of the local competition will move on to the regional competition.

    Lisa won the local competition.

    ∴ Lisa will be going to the regional competition.

"Jabberwocky" and the Ultimate Syllogism Practice

Perhaps you used "common sense" to help you complete the practice exercises. People often look at syllogisms and say "I can just tell when they are valid and when they are invalid."

This practice will challenge your "syllogism skills." This practice is based on Lewis Carroll's "Jabberwocky," a famous poem composed of a lot of nonsense words that, when it is read, makes perfectly good sense. (See Chapter 3 on induction and the "rules" of grammar.)

Carroll's poem reveals how common patterns (not really "rules") give sense to our language, even when the individual words are gibberish.

DEDUCTIVE REASONING

Read Carroll's famous poem just for fun. After you read the poem, move on to the Jabberwocky practice syllogisms, and test the validity of each syllogism using the "conditions/consequences" rules that you have learned.

Jabberwocky

by Lewis Carroll (Charles L. Dodgson)
from *Through the Looking-Glass* (1871)

'Twas brillig, and the slithy toves
  Did gyre and gimble in the wabe:
All mimsy were the borogoves,
  And the mome raths outgrabe.

"Beware the Jabberwock, my son!
  The jaws that bite, the claws that catch!
Beware the Jubjub bird, and shun
  The frumious Bandersnatch!"

He took his vorpal sword in hand:
  Long time the manxome foe he sought—
So rested he by the Tumtum tree,
  And stood awhile in thought.

And, as in uffish thought he stood,
  The Jabberwock, with eyes of flame,
Came whiffling through the tulgey wood,
  And burbled as it came!

One two! One two! And through and through
  The vorpal blade went snicker-snack!
He left it dead, and with its head
  He went galumphing back.

"And hast thou slain the Jabberwock?
  Come to my arms, my beamish boy!
O frabjous day! Callooh! Callay!"
  He chortled in his joy.

'Twas brillig, and the slithy toves
  Did gyre and gimble in the wabe:
All mimsy were the borogoves,
  And the mome raths outgrabe.

Practice 5.d. Working with syllogisms: The nonsense approach!

Directions: Use the "conditions/consequences" rules to test the validity of these syllogisms. Most of the nouns and adjectives in the syllogisms are nonsense words from "Jabberwocky." You will have to truly rely on the four rules presented earlier in this chapter to determine validity.

1. All slithes are toves.

    The wabe is a tove.

    ∴ The wabe is a slithe.

2. All slithes are toves.

    The mimsy is a slithe.

    ∴ The mimsy is a tove.

3. All borogoves are brillig.

    The Bandersnatch is not a borogove.

    ∴ The borogove is not brillig.

4. All momraths are vorpals.

    The frume is not a vorpal.

    ∴ The frume is not a momrath.

5. All borogroves are brilig.

    The gyre is brillig.

    ∴ The gyre is a borogove.

6. Toves are foolish.

    The beamish boy was a tove.

    ∴ The beamish boy was foolish.

7. The jabberwock was frabjous.

    The callay was frabjous.

    ∴ The callay was a jabberwock.

8. The jaws were slithy.

    The claws were slithy.

    ∴ The jaws were claws.

9. Jubjub birds are brillig.

   The tove is not a Jubjub bird.

   ∴ The tove is not brillig.

10. All foes of the beamish boy are Bandersnatches.

    The narrator of the poem is not a Bandersnatch.

    ∴ The narrator of the poem is not a foe of the beamish boy.

Hopefully, you made some sense out of Lewis Carroll's nonsense poem. Your new skills in evaluating syllogisms should be revealed as you work through Practice 5.d. Be sure to check your answers at the back of the book.

Syllogisms and Political Arguments

It is not uncommon for politicians to use syllogistic argument forms. Like lawyers speaking to a jury, they often try to thread the syllogism into everyday speech. Now that you have some experience in syllogistic reasoning, you will recognize the pattern when it appears in ordinary conversation or in a speech. As you form the pattern in your mind, you can test the validity of the speaker's statements. This is an especially valuable skill in separating the rhetoric of a speech from the strength of the arguments.

Here is a practice exercise based on an everyday conversation:

> My neighbor says to me, "Well, you know Mr Smith, our friend down the street, is supporting Mr Bush, and the Republican Party."
>
> "How do you know?" I asked.
>
> "Well, we know that supporters of the Bush candidacy also support gun ownership. I saw Mr Jones going hunting with his son last week, and he owns his own gun. It's easy to see that Mr Jones must support the Bush candidacy."

How does this look in syllogistic form?

> Supporters of the Bush candidacy also support gun ownership.
>
> Mr Jones supports gun ownership.
>
> ∴ Mr Jones supports the Bush candidacy.

You might try this one on your friends. Some will nod vigorously in agreement: "Yes, that's so," they are thinking. It will take a person with your reasoning skills to say, "Wait, not necessarily. You should not affirm the consequence!"

Reasoning by Either/Or

Another common type of deductive reasoning is reasoning by either/or. My favorite weatherman uses it all the time; "Either it will rain or it won't." This is a simple, seemingly "no fail" type of reasoning, which is why people are so fond of it.

Here is a practical example: You are applying for a part-time job at the neighborhood grocery store. You have just walked into the neighborhood store and the owner gives you an application form that says, "Please type or print." You want to apply right there at the store, so you decide to print on the form.

Either/or is simple, but in order for it to be valid, two conditions must be met:

Rule 1: The two possibilities must be **exclusive**. This means they must only exist separately; they can't both exist at the same time.

In the example above, you can't print *and* type your information on the form; you do one or the other. The weather prediction is silly, but it's valid: It can't rain and not rain at the same time.

People can be so conditioned to making choices that they forget that sometimes, they could have both. Recently, two friends sitting in a cafe were debating: Should we have iced water or coffee with our dessert? It was warm, and iced water sounded good, but a leisurely cup of coffee sounded good also. While one friend was struggling to decide, the other friend ordered both. "Please bring me a glass of iced water," she said, "and also a cup of coffee." The other friend said, "I never thought of ordering both!" This casual example is just a reminder that not all choices are exclusive. When presented with the words "either/or," always check.

Note: You may hear the phrase **mutually exclusive** to indicate that only one possibility can exist at one time. This popular phrase is rather redundant; for our purposes, the single word **exclusive** will do.

Rule 2: The two possibilities must be **exhaustive**. That means there can't be third possibility.

In the example above about filling out the form, the applicant should not fill in his or her answers with cursive writing; it is not one of the choices. Besides being "exclusive" (you can only do one or the other), the available choices are also "exhaustive" – printing or typing are the only two possible choices.

In the restaurant example, there are even more choices than the two provided. Any restaurant patron could have water, coffee, iced tea, soda, milk… the list contains more than two choices. This is important, because people often set up artificial "choices" between two things when there are a number of options.

Here is a similar example: In a cafeteria line, a mother says to her child, "You can have white milk or chocolate." But even a very young child may notice immediately that his or her mother hasn't given all the choices: There is also both juice and soda in the cafeteria drink selection. In this example, the choices are **not exhaustive**. The mother has determined that she wants to allow the child only the two milk choices, but really, there are a number of possibilities.

This is important: The strong reasoner asks if there are truly only two choices, and looks for the possibility of a third or even fourth choice before coming to a conclusion.

Why does the rule of "choices must be exhaustive" matter? Because people who feel strongly about an issue often set up false either/or situations. Here is an example:

> A parent warns his child, "You can either go to university or dig ditches the rest of your life."

Parents often try this type of scare tactic to keep their children on an educational track, but in fact, there are a lot of options open, not just those two.

In the language of logic, the two choices are **not exhaustive**. In the political world, politicians like to say things like, "We can either spend our money on education or on health care," or to provide similar options. Quite often, with careful money management, it is possible to do both and pay for other programs, too. Don't be caught up in an either/or choice without checking.

Assuming there are only two choices, and that a choice must be made, is called **faulty dilemma**. Be wary. Always ask yourself, "Could we choose both? Could there be a third possibility?"

Reasoning by If/Then

In this type of reasoning, we suggest that if certain conditions are met, a necessary result will follow.

Example: "If you go out into the rain, you will get wet." You go out into the rain, and you do get wet.

This makes sense. Most reasoning by if/then is fairly straightforward. The problem with if/then is the temptation to reverse the process. This will not work.

You will notice that the **converse** is not necessarily true: "You got wet; therefore you must have gone out in the rain." It's not valid because you might have gotten wet some other way.

Also, much like classic syllogistic reasoning, if/then reasoning is only workable when the major premise is true. Thus, the two rules for if/then reasoning are:

> **Rule 1:** Check to make sure that the first statement (the major premise) is inherently true.
>
> **Rule 2:** The converse of an if/then is not usually valid.

Both if/then and either/or are simple, everyday forms of reasoning. You don't have to study logic to use them. But a serious study of logic can show us when they are used correctly and when they are not. You will see some practice exercises for if/then and either/or in the review questions for this chapter.

Chapter Review

1. Determine whether this if/then reasoning is valid:

    If my mortgage is approved, I can buy that house. My mortgage application was approved. Now I can go ahead and buy the house!

2. Deduction is also called _____.

3. A diagram of concentric circles that shows the relationship between classes is called a _____.

4. A three-part formal argument is called a _____.

5. The first item in the major premise is the _____.

6. The second item, or second half, of the major premise is called the _____.

DEDUCTIVE REASONING

7. Valid means _____.

8. Determine the validity of this either/or line of reasoning: We decided to eat at the new restaurant in town. The waiter explained the restaurant's policy. Either we could order the *prix fixe* dinner, or we could order individual items *à la carte*. We didn't like the *prix fixe* menu, so we ordered *à la carte*.

9. Valid or invalid: If there is a weather-related cancellation at school, a lot of students will be at the mall. I saw some students at the mall today, so classes must have been cancelled because of the inclement weather.

10. List the four rules for syllogism validity that we learned in this chapter.

6

ERRORS IN REASONING: THE CLASSICAL FALLACIES

People use logic and reasoning in mathematics and the sciences. Working through a line of reasoning is a natural part of those fields.

Thinking and talking logically in the everyday world can be quite a challenge, as we have already seen. The purpose of this text is to reveal the reasoning process used as we develop supportable positions on social and political issues, and when we make decisions in everyday life. This chapter is devoted to the thinking skills you need to analyze the persuasive discussions around you.

You have already been presented with several ways in which reasoning can go wrong. It is common to make mistakes in the reasoning process. In addition to the types of "process" errors you have learned about, there are other common types of reasoning errors. A number of these errors have been grouped together under the heading of "The Fallacies." All of them typically happen in ordinary conversations, in advertisements, in political speeches, and in print and electronic media.

These reasoning errors were studied, categorized and named over two thousand years ago by the Greeks, and then the Romans, who made the first formal studies of logic.

Many of these "fallacies" are still referred to today by their Latin names.

A Note about Propaganda: Propaganda is a well-known term for the systematic dissemination of a belief or an agenda. Propaganda has taken on a negative connotation; when we feel that someone is trying to pressure us to believe something, we call it "propaganda." We sense that the thinking is wrong, but we might not be able to analyze why this is the case. The key lies in recognizing the common fallacies. Recognizing the fallacies in speeches and journalism is one way to deflate the hot air of propaganda.

In Chapter 6, you will be introduced to a number of the fallacies. To help you understand them better, they have been grouped into two categories: fallacies of process and fallacies about people.

Classical Fallacies of Processing Information

In Chapters 4 and 5, we looked at the process of reasoning. We studied **induction** and **deduction** to understand the basic processes of moving through a line of reasoning. Additional errors in processing information happen so often that they are identified as **classical fallacies**. We should try to avoid them, and beware of people who use them intentionally. Let's look at the 12 process fallacies:

1. **Hasty Generalization:** This was discussed in the section on induction. It happens when we make a generalization based on too few examples. This is such a common mistake in reasoning that we have an ordinary expression – **jumping to conclusions** – to identify this error.

2. **Begging the Question:** This happens when the arguer weaves a statement that **needs to be proven** into the proposition as if it were already accepted as fact.

Imagine being asked the following question: "Do you still cheat on tests?"

What would your answer be? It only takes a moment to realize that, no matter what you say, you will look guilty of cheating. Even if your answer is "No, of course not," you have fallen into a trap: The word *still* implies that you did cheat in the past. There is no way out of this one – unless, of course, you can say to your accuser, "You're begging the question."

Begging the question has been a classic tactic of lawyers trying to discredit a witness. The lawyer asks, "Mr Jones, do you still cheat on your income tax?" It doesn't matter if Mr Jones refuses to answer, or if the judge denies the question. The lawyer as already planted the seed in the jury's mind. By "begging the question," or not proving that Mr Jones used to cheat on his taxes, he has quietly made the witness look bad.

Early in Chapter 2 we touched on **begging the question** when we discussed writing a good proposition. Here is the example we looked at in Chapter 2:

"The *inadequate* library facilities should be improved."

If the facilities are inadequate, there is no argument; of course they need to be improved. But that hasn't been proven yet; the arguer must show that the facilities are inadequate as part of the reasoning behind improving them. The proposition should read:

> "The library facilities should be improved."

Now that the proposition has been improved by removing the error of begging the question, we are ready to move on with the pros and cons.

A fair investigation of an issue begins with a fair statement of the argument. Remember not to allow any unsupported contentions into a proposition.

Note: In the world of debate, **question** means **issue,** or the point being argued. In the above examples, it is appropriate to say that the words "inadequate" and "still" have been **begged.**

Begging the Question – Circular Argument: Arguing in a circle is a form of begging the question. Here's an example:

> "Joe Smith is a great up-and-coming football player."
>
> "Who told you that?"
>
> "My Uncle George."
>
> "How does he know?"
>
> "Well, he knows who all of the best players are, and he said Joe Smith was one of them."

This weak process will go around and around – creating a **circular argument** – with no clarifying explanation. It is not good reasoning.

3. **Ignoring the Question** – is just that. When faced with a major premise you cannot refute, you ignore it and try to change the subject.

   > Mother says, "Oh, dear! This is terrible. You failed your literature exam this semester."
   >
   > The young student says, "But I got A's in science!"
   >
   > Or, the young student says, "Father says he never did well in literature."
   >
   > Or, he complains about his sibling: "Leslie did poorly in science and you never said one word to her!"

All of the young student's responses are examples of "ignoring the question." Any statement that the student uses to get the mother to stop thinking about his or her poor results in literature and transfer her attention to a different argument is a distraction that may help the student get out of an uncomfortable spot. But these comments do not respond to the issue at hand: the poor grade.

Providing a distracter is also called a **red herring**. The **red herring** is a popular ruse in the classic detective stories of Agatha Christie and Arthur Conan Doyle. Modern writers, as well as both fictional and real detectives, often deal with these distracters. Now you can look for them, too.

A Note about "The Straw Man" Fallacy: The "Straw Man" argument is an extension of both **begging the question** and **ignoring the question**. The arguer creates a "Straw Man," or an imaginary problem that includes the emotional language associated with begging the question to ignore the question, i.e., to deflect the opposition's attention away from the actual question at hand.

4. **Equivocation:** This fallacy is using the same word or phrase in two different ways, purposefully hiding or changing one of the meanings.

Perhaps the most famous literary equivocators are the witches in Shakespeare's *Macbeth*. The witches "equivocate" with Macbeth by showing prophecies that seem favorable in the way he sees them, but are unfavorable in the way that the witches mean them. Macbeth's inability to see their charade is his ultimate undoing. He refuses to see a potential attack, because the witches have told him he can never be harmed until "Birnham Woods comes to Dunsinane." Macbeth takes that to mean "never" because, in his mind, the forest cannot march up to his castle. Unfortunately, Malcolm's army has cut up branches from the trees in Birnham Wood to cover themselves as camouflage as they march on Macbeth's castle. It is not until one of his castle guards calls out "The woods are marching," that Macbeth realizes the witches have duped him.

In a modern, everyday setting, a teenager might say to his father,

> "Father, you wouldn't scold me for something I didn't do, would you?"
>
> "Of course not," says Father.
>
> "That's a relief!" says the young man. "I didn't do my chores!"

Now, it is easy to see that two different concepts have emerged from the phrase "something I didn't do." The father was thinking, "I wouldn't scold my son if he didn't do anything wrong," but the son actually uses the words "something I didn't do" to disguise his neglect.

A common error is using the word "law" two different ways in the same argument. "Law" should not be used to mean both natural law and government law in the same argument.

A Note about Definition: An important start to any debate or argument is the "Definition of Terms." Those who are involved in the debate should agree to define important terms at the beginning of the argument in order to avoid any hint of equivocation. The entire debate should proceed with the given definitions in mind.

The euthanasia or physician-assisted suicide issue is a strong case in point. When this controversial issue is brought up, the word "murder" often surfaces, and arguers on both sides often think that this is an easy word that everyone understands. But when we think about it, we realize that a nation does not accuse its soldiers of murder, and that proven self-defense is not considered murder. To move forward in this debate, both sides must establish a legal and/or ethical definition of the word. In this situation, determining the actual definition may be so important that it becomes one of the "issues." (See Chapter 2.)

5. **Post Hoc/Propter Hoc:** This error is the result of confused cause and effect.

> "Every time I plan a fun weekend, I am assigned an extra project at work and have to cancel my plans. I think just planning to have fun makes my boss give me more work!"

Most people would see this as silly thinking. But people have seen "causes" for health problems in a similar way; a brief look at the history of cancer investigation will show that items such as cranberries and aspirin, which are currently considered safe, and even healthy, were thought to cause cancer.

In a similar vein, consider this possibility:

> "All cocaine addicts drank milk when they were babies. Therefore, we can assume that drinking milk leads to cocaine addiction."

If you think no one would believe this, look at this similar example: People who use crack used to use marijuana. Therefore, marijuana use obviously leads to crack use. What does the data say? How many people use marijuana and do not become crack/cocaine users? This is a current concern that has the data crunchers working overtime because the issue of "gateway drugs" has important implications for our society. The concept of "gateway drugs" relies on a perceived cause and effect relationship that suggests that using marijuana leads to using cocaine. People on the other side of the argument, such as those who would like marijuana to be legal for medicinal purposes, suggest that the cause and effect relationship has not been established; more study is warranted.

The point is, just because one thing happens before another, this does not mean the former caused the latter. It is important to review carefully all the available information before assigning a "cause." Readers of this text who have taken a statistics course will remember this concept: positive correlation does not mean a causal relationship.

6. **Non Sequitur:** "It does not follow." This means that the "conclusion" is not really the logical result of the premises. Take a look at this example: "John Jones does not drink or smoke. I'm sure he will make a good president." This is not good thinking; a person's personal habits have very little to do with his qualifications for holding an office. His good personal health habits will not necessarily lead to good leadership.

7. **Dicto Simpliciter:** Using an unqualified generalization to support a belief. "Milk is good; therefore everyone should drink milk." An old saying that emphasizes dicto simpliciter goes like this: "All generalizations are bad, including this one."

8. **Contradictory Premises:** This happens when the main premises contradict each other. It presents a "no win" situation that is inconsistent with logic. The classic example of this one is "Could God create a stone so big he couldn't lift it?" There is no way out of this one: if God could create the stone, then he could not lift it. If he could lift it, he couldn't create the stone. People who create contradictory premises are often smug about their success in proving their point, but a strong reasoner will rely on evidence and reliable processing methods, not contradictory premises.

9. **Hypothesis Contrary to Fact:** The arguer tries to draw a conclusion from what did not happen. This is unrealistic, since no one knows what might have happened had the circumstances been different. A common example is looking at our own lives and saying "I wouldn't be here today (in college, in this job, in this relationship) if I hadn't (met you on the bus,

lost my keys that day, answered that phone call)." Many paths lead to the same destination; we just don't know what would have happened if the timelines of our lives had been different. We do know that a different path wouldn't necessarily preclude our being where we are today.

10. **Fallacies of Composition and Division:** These are two separate fallacies, but they are closely related. We should not make an assumption about a group based on one item, nor should we make assumptions about an item based on a group. For example, a football team may be the best team in the league, but that does not mean their goalie is the best in the league (**fallacy of division**). In the same way, a player may be named the best goalie in the league, but it would not be logical to assume to that his team is therefore the best team in the league (**fallacy of composition**).

11. **Faulty Dilemma:** The process error of faulty dilemma happens when the speaker suggests that there are only two choices when actually there are other possibilities. "We can either spend our tax dollars on the poor or on defense." (See the section on either/or reasoning in Chapter 5. Faulty dilemma is actually the reasoning error of major premises being **not exhaustive**.)

In politics, faulty dilemma is often preceded by the phrase, "Our choice is clear...", after which the speaker presents us with the "lesser of two evils": "We can join this conflict now, or lose all of our freedoms tomorrow." If the "choice is clear," it may not be. Look closely.

12. **The Parade of Horrors/The Slippery Slope**: This line of thinking suggests that if we allow a situation to happen once, it will grow into a big problem or happen more often. This is a special type of cause and effect thinking that doesn't hold up under scrutiny. Typically, this fallacy is heard when people are talking about behavior. Here is an example: A neighborhood watch sees a child out at 10:03, just after curfew hour of 10:00 p.m. One member of the neighborhood team complains, "Nothing was done. We have to enforce the rules. Before you know it, we will have teens all over the neighborhood at midnight, making noise and disturbing everyone." There is actually little evidence that a small, occasional infraction leads to serious problems. If you need to examine a "slippery slope" concern, ask to see data from similar situations before overreacting.

Note: Review Chapter 3 on evidence for an explanation of another common fallacy involving multiple facts on one side of an argument, the fallacy of **stacking the deck**.

Firm up your skills in recognizing the common process fallacies by doing the practice exercises, and listen actively for fallacies the next time you hear a speech or see an advertisement.

Practice 6.a. Process fallacies at a town meeting

Directions: Sit in on this imaginary town meeting. A local citizen, Mr Brown, is asking the Town Council to repair his street. While he is talking, he makes a few classic errors in reasoning. Examine each numbered item and identify the fallacy from the list of process fallacies you have just studied.

> "Mr Mayor and council members," begins Mr Brown. "It is high time the City Council repaired the dangerous pavement on Elm Street. (1) The city has only two choices at this point, either to repair Elm Street or to face a lawsuit from someone whose car is damaged driving on this street. (2) A city should be proud of its streets; it should keep things in good repair. And if Elm Street is neglected, it won't be long before every street in our town is in disrepair. (3) At the last Town Council meeting, I asked you to address this concern, and Councilman Jeffers asked, 'Where will we get the money for these repairs?' Well, I ask you, Mr Mayor and Council Members, where will we get the money for trash pick-up? (4) This situation is just like last month's problem with our streetlights. If Mr Adams hadn't come to the meeting and complained, nothing would ever have been done!" (5)

Classical Fallacies about People and Personalities

A common tendency of the human mind is to combine our social interactions with our reasoning processes. As a result, discussions of people and their behaviors can contain reasoning errors. This group of fallacies shows how we can easily be swayed by our emotions and interactions with the people around us.

1. **Argumentum ad Hominem:** A person argues against a person instead of a point, maintaining that a point is bad because a "bad" person believes in it. "Don't support Senator B's current proposal… Remember, he's the married senator who was seen with another woman." Attacking the senator's behavior becomes, if we allow it, an attack on the senator's legislative proposal. Personal attacks are inappropriate.

Name calling and comments like "Only an idiot would believe that," are forms of **ad hominem**. This is sometimes called **poisoning the well**.

2. **Ad Misericordiam:** This can be translated as an **appeal to pity**. Trying to make someone feel sorry for others is a good way to get your opponent's mind off the logical progression of argument. It is very effective, but it is not good reasoning.

   In a recent discussion about vaccines given to small children, one mother was heard saying, "I won't have my child get all those shots! It is so mean; she cries and cries." Well, no one wants to see a crying child, but if the vaccines are safe and effective, it would seem worth a few tears to protect the child. The argument, then, is about safety and effectiveness, not about our sympathy for a child who cries at the doctor's office.

3. **Appeal to Popular Opinion:** This is sometimes called **getting on the bandwagon**. The promoter of an idea says, "Everyone thinks" or "Everyone is doing it," hoping the listener will be persuaded to go along with the group. This is a popular form of persuasion, but again, it is not good reasoning. In Latin this is called **ad populum**. The **plain folks** appeal is another form of ad populum. The speaker appeals not only to popular opinion, but to the opinion of the ordinary person, or "everyman." This method is employed to gain approval for an idea by making it appear humble. Politicians are adept at this technique as they campaign, shake hands and try to act like the average voter. The representative who doesn't want to raise taxes will parry the opposition's threat to raise them by saying "A tax increase will hurt people like you and me." Once elected, the politician probably will lead a life very different from that of the average man, but he will try to appear "average" to get the votes.

4. **Appeal to Force:** Direct or implied threats are often used to convince people to adopt a certain opinion. This is not good reasoning. Most people realize that they should not be victimized by threats of physical violence, but subtler threats are harder to recognize. For example, companies often respond to workers' requests to unionize by saying, "When the company accedes to union demands, it becomes more expensive for the company. Now, we don't really care if you workers unionize, but just remember, there may be some job losses afterwards." This is a politely spoken, veiled threat: The company has suggested that, if the workers form a union, the company will cut jobs. This quiet threat is enough to make many union supporters back down.

5. **Ad Verecundiam:** This fallacy is an **appeal to authority**. See the section on evidence in Chapter 3 for more explanation on both the appropriate

and inappropriate ways to use the voice of authority, reliable sources and expert opinions. Key ideas include selecting authorities that are truly versed in the particular field of inquiry, and not transferring authority to popular or powerful people who are speaking outside of their realm of knowledge.

6. **Tu Quoque:** This can be translated as "And you, too." This is the arguer's tendency to push an accusation back at the accuser. "My doctor said I should give up smoking, but I told him that he should quit, too," or "Why can't I be late for work? The boss doesn't come in until 10:00 a.m." The tu quoque argument makes very little sense: In the smoking example, we know that smoking is bad for one's health, and if a person has breathing problems or other issues clearly related to smoking, the individual should try to quit. It doesn't matter whether the doctor smokes or not. And while we may wish the boss kept the same long hours that we do, we may have to live with the reality that, to keep our jobs, we have to come to work on time without complaint.

Recognizing the fallacies about people and personalities may first have the effect of making us change our own speech habits. Reasoners who have studied the personal fallacies are less likely to make personal attacks, and less likely to respond with a "you, too" response when they are asked to work harder or longer, or to eat fewer calories.

Good thinkers are also less likely to allow others to make personal attacks, or speak with veiled threats. To strengthen understanding of the personal fallacies, complete the practice exercises below.

Practice 6.b. Practice with fallacies

Directions: Read each of these vignettes and identify the fallacy in reasoning.

1. Should the EU bail out the Greek economy? I think not. Before you know it, the EU will have to bail out every country in the group.
2. The government should allow euthanasia. After all, euthanasia means "Good Death," so it would be a good law.
3. Don't let Bill drive! Did you ever see how messy his garage is?
4. My dentist said that 5- and 6-year-olds should have their first dental checkup, but I don't think so. Imagine those poor little kids trembling at the thought of going to the dentist. It is just too sad.

5. Yes, I met my husband at the bus stop one rainy day. Imagine, if it hadn't been raining that day, we never would have met.

6. The students ask the teacher to change the day of the test. "Okay," Mr Higgins agrees, "I can change the day. But we might cover more material by then; I can't promise that the test will be as easy as the one I have planned for Monday."

7. How can you explain this foolishness? Have you always been this careless?

8. Our choice is clear! We can hire all new teachers or live with these antiquated education theories!

9. If the North hadn't won the Civil War, we would still have slavery in the United States.

10. My doctor said I should lose a few pounds. Well, he's at least fifty pounds overweight himself; it must not be that big a deal!

REASONING THROUGH THE AGES

The Context of Argument: Logos, Ethos and Pathos

The early Greeks acknowledged the complexity of the human mind and its capacity to engage in debate. Aristotle and others studied not only the ability to create a line of reasoning, but also the manner in which people interact and appeal to each other in debate.

Aristotle identified and defined three appeals: **logos**, **ethos** and **pathos**.

The chapters on **induction** and **deduction** focus on the **logos** of argument, as in the word "logic." We appeal to the mind's ability to follow a line of reasoning. Formal, academic argument relies most generally on an appeal to logos.

At the same time, we like to think that a person presenting a "reasonable" argument is also acting ethically, that we can respect this person's commitment to honesty and goodwill. Aristotle called this appeal **ethos**, and it is represented in the public attitude toward great statesmen like Patrick Henry and Martin Luther King, Jr. Strong speakers who appeal to ethos will avoid many of the personal fallacies mentioned in the previous chapter. A strong speaker will want the audience to know that he or she is speaking from a point of honesty and transparency.

The third appeal is **pathos**. No doubt you can see the base "pathos" in our familiar words "sympathy" and "empathy." Pathos in argument can be seen in our modern concept of empathy, the idea that we can all identify with the common feelings and needs of humanity.

While formal argument follows the lines of inductive and deductive reasoning, all human persuasion includes ethos and pathos along with logos; it is just part of human nature.

Review this classic speech by Patrick Henry, presented in 1775. You may have already heard the resounding end to this speech, "Give me Liberty or give me death." Examining the beginning of this speech will reveal Henry's purposeful appeals to logos, ethos and pathos. Each appeal is noted with underlines and notations.

> *Patrick Henry's Speech to the Virginia Convention* (March 1775)
>
> *No man thinks more highly than I do of the patriotism, as well as the abilities, of the very worthy gentlemen who have just addressed the House. But different men often see the same subject in different lights, and I hope it will not be thought disrespectful to those gentlemen, if, entertaining as I do, opinions of a character very opposite to theirs, I shall speak freely and without reserve.* [These first two sentences establish **ethos**, Henry's commitment to a *fair-minded approach* to the subject.] *The question before the House is one of awful moment to this country. For my part, I consider it as nothing less than a question of freedom or slavery.* [In these two sentences, Henry appeals to **pathos**, compelling his audience to feel the urgency of the moment, a sense of patriotism, and concern for the citizenry.] *And in proportion to the magnitude of the subject ought to be the freedom of debate.* [In this final moment of introduction, Henry appeals to **logos**, asking his audience to approach the subject logically and with a clear call to fair debate.]

Not every speech will display these three appeals so clearly and directly, but Patrick Henry, like many modern orators such as Winston Churchill and Martin Luther King, Jr, was a serious student of argument, persuasion and debate.

The Context of Argument: Two Modern Approaches

Two modern thinkers affected the study of logic and argument by looking at the Greek standards of persuasion and formulating ideas that fit with our modern environment.

Carl R. Rogers (1902–1987), an American psychologist, formulated an approach to argument that acknowledges the commonality or shared beliefs of the two sides. In Rogerian discussion, the writer or speaker would make the effort to acknowledge that both sides should be respected, and that one's opponent has a valid point of view. In focusing on this common ground, the Rogerian might even withhold his or her position or proposition until the end of the debate, allowing the opposition to see that it benefits everyone to accept the author's position. While Rogerian argument is often seen as the opposite of Aristotelian dialogue, many thinkers feel that Rogers was ultimately trying to respect our human needs for ethos, as the speaker presents himself or herself as a fair and open person, and pathos, as the speaker shares the values of those on the other side of the debate.

Another important thinker of the twentieth century was the British philosopher Stephen E. Toulmin (1922–2009), who strove to identify humanism in modern debate. Toulmin changed the vocabulary of debate, giving us the words "warrants," "claims," "grounds" and "qualifiers" to provide a new model for the debate process.

Toulmin allowed an interconnectedness of ideas, rather that the absolute, forward, linear process that is often associated with Aristotelian logic.

Most twenty-first century thinkers – theorists, politicians and journalists – incorporate all three studies of logical thinking as they construct their arguments. When you reach Chapter 8 of this book and work on a persuasive project of your own, you will be encouraged to provide some sense of common ground as you introduce your argument, and to acknowledge respectfully the other side as you allow the complexity of your own debate topic to emerge. In doing so, you are including the concepts of both Rogers and Toulmin. This text concentrates on an introduction to the skills needed to formulate a traditional argument. If you want to continue in your study of logic and language, you will want to investigate the persuasive processes of these two modern thinkers and add their concepts to your repertoire.

The Context of Argument: A Literary Approach

Literature puts the daily arguments of human life into a creative presentation. We use the word "conflict" to describe the essence of plot and action in a story. In this chapter, we'll take a look at several classic examples of argument and persuasion in the ongoing tale of human interaction.

Marlow's "The Passionate Shepherd to His Love" and Raleigh's "The Nymph's Reply to the Shepherd" remind us that the true Renaissance man was both a poet and a rational thinker. Another Elizabethan piece, "To the Virgins, to Make Much of Time" shows how people – even people in love – like to think logically and sensibly.

But first, since we've just finished a chapter on the Greek fallacies, we'll start with a delightfully funny modern short story entitled "Love is a Fallacy" by

Max Schulman. Imagine yourself on a university campus in the first year of your studies, and enjoy this story of Polly, the first-year beauty who becomes a student of logic.

Love is a Fallacy

by Max Shulman

Cool was I, and logical. Keen, calculating, perspicacious, acute and astute – I was all of these. My brain was as powerful as a dynamo, as precise as a chemist's scales, as penetrating as a scalpel. And – think of it! – I was only eighteen.

It is not often that one so young has such a giant intellect. Take for example, Petey Butch, my roommate at the University of Minnesota. Same age, same background, but dumb as an ox. A nice enough fellow, you understand, but nothing upstairs. Emotional type. Unstable. Impressionable. Worst of all, a faddist. Fads, I submit, are the very negation of reason. To be swept up in every new craze that comes along, to surrender yourself to idiocy just because everybody else is doing it – this, to me, is the acme of mindlessness. Not, however, to Petey.

One afternoon I found Petey lying on his bed with an expression of such distress on his face that I immediately diagnosed appendicitis. "Don't move," I said. "Don't take a laxative. I'll get a doctor."

"Raccoon," he mumbled thickly.

"Raccoon?" I said, pausing in my flight.

"I want a raccoon coat," he wailed.

I perceived that his trouble was not physical, but mental. "Why do you want a raccoon coat?"

"I should have known it," he cried, pounding his temples. "I should have known they'd come back when the Charleston came back. Like a fool I spent all my money on textbooks, and now I can't get a raccoon coat."

"Can you mean," I said incredulously, "that people are actually wearing raccoon coats again?"

"All the Big Men on Campus are wearing them. Where have you been?"

"In the library," I said, naming a place not frequented by Big Men on Campus.

He leaped from the bed and paced the room. "I've got to have a raccoon coat," he said passionately. "I've got to!"

"Petey, why? Look at it rationally. Raccoon coats are unsanitary. They shed. They smell bad. They weigh too much. They're unsightly. They– "

"You don't understand," he interrupted impatiently. "It's the thing to do. Don't you want to be in the swim?"

"No," I said truthfully.

"Well, I do," he declared. "I'd give anything for a raccoon coat. Anything!"

My brain, that precision instrument, slipped into high gear. "Anything?" I asked, looking at him narrowly.

"Anything," he affirmed in ringing tones.

I stroked my chin thoughtfully. It so happened that I knew where to get my hands on a raccoon coat. My father had had one in his undergraduate days; it lay now in a trunk in the attic back home. It also happened that Petey had something I wanted. He didn't have it exactly, but at least he had first rights on it. I refer to his girl, Polly Espy.

I had long coveted Polly Espy. Let me emphasize that my desire for this young woman was not emotional in nature. She was, to be sure, a girl who excited the emotions, but I was not one to let my heart rule my head. I wanted Polly for a shrewdly calculated, entirely cerebral reason.

I was a freshman in law school. In a few years I would be out in practice. I was well aware of the importance of the right kind of wife in furthering a lawyer's career. The successful lawyers I had observed were, almost without exception, married to beautiful, gracious, intelligent women. With one omission, Polly fitted these specifications perfectly.

Beautiful she was. She was not yet of pin-up proportions, but I felt sure that time would supply the lack. She already had the makings.

Gracious she was. By gracious I mean full of graces. She had an erectness of carriage, an ease of bearing, a poise that clearly indicated the best of breeding. At table her manners were exquisite. I had seen her at the Kozy Kampus Korner eating the specialty of the house – a sandwich that contained scraps of pot roast, gravy chopped nuts, and a dipper of sauerkraut – without even getting her fingers moist.

Intelligent she was not. In fact, she veered in the opposite direction. But I believed that under my guidance she would smarten up. At any rate, it was worth a try. It is, after all, easier to make a beautiful dumb girl smart than to make an ugly smart girl beautiful.

"Petey," I said, "are you in love with Polly Espy?"

"I think she's a keen kid," he replied, "but I don't know if you'd call it love. Why?"

"Do you," I asked, "have any kind of formal arrangement with her? I mean are you going steady or anything like that?"

"No. We see each other quite a bit, but we both have other dates. Why?"

"Is there," I asked, "any other man for whom she has a particular fondness?"

"Not that I know of. Why?"

I nodded with satisfaction. "In other words, if you were out of the picture, the field would be open. Is that right?"

"I guess so. What are you getting at?"

"Nothing, nothing," I said innocently, and took my suitcase out of the closet.

"Where are you going?" asked Petey.

"Home for the weekend." I threw a few things into the bag.

"Listen," he said, clutching my arm eagerly. "While you're home, you couldn't get some money from your old man, could you, and lend it to me so I can buy a raccoon coat?"

"I may do better than that," I said with a mysterious wink and closed my bag and left.

"Look," I said to Petey when I got back Monday morning. I threw open the suitcase and revealed the huge, hairy, gamy object that my father had worn in his Stutz Bearcat in 1925.

"Holy Toledo!" said Petey reverently. He plunged his hands into the raccoon coat and then his face. "Holy Toledo," he repeated fifteen or twenty times.

"Would you like it?" I asked.

"Oh yes!" he cried, clutching the greasy pelt to him. Then a canny look came into his eyes. "What do you want for it?"

"Your girl," I said, mincing no words.

"Polly?" he said in a horrified whisper. "You want Polly?"

"That's right."

He flung the coat from him. "Never," he said stoutly.

I shrugged. "Okay. If you don't want to be in the swim, I guess it's your business."

I sat down in a chair and pretended to read a book, but out of the corner of my eye I kept watching Petey. He was a torn man. First he looked at the coat with the expression of a waif at a baker's window. Then he turned away and set his jaw resolutely. Then he looked back at the coat, with even more longing in his face. Then he turned away, but with not so much resolution this time. Back and forth his head swiveled, desire waxing, resolution waning. Finally he didn't turn away at all; he just stood and stared with mad lust at the coat.

"It isn't as though I was in love with Polly," he said thickly. "Or going steady or anything like that."

"That's right," I murmured.

"What's Polly to me, or me to Polly?"

"Not a thing," said I.

"It's just been a causal kick – just a few laughs, that's all."

"Try on the coat," said I.

He complied. The coat bunched high over his ears and dropped all the way down to his shoe tops. He looked like a mound of dead raccoons. "Fits fine," he said happily.

I rose from my chair. "Is it a deal?" I asked, extending my hand. He swallowed. "It's a deal," he said and shook my hand.

I had my first date with Polly the following evening. This was in the nature of a survey; I wanted to find out just how much work I had to do to get her mind up to the standard I required. I took her first to dinner. "Gee, that was a delish dinner," she said as we left the restaurant. Then I took her to a movie. "Gee, that was a marvy movie," she said as we left the theater. And then I took her home. "Gee, I had a sensaysh time," she said as she bade me good night.

I went back to my room with a heavy heart. I had gravely underestimated the size of my task. This girl's lack of information was terrifying. Nor would it be enough merely to supply her with information. First she had to be taught to think. This loomed as a project of no small dimensions, and at first I was tempted to give her back to Petey. But then I got to thinking about her abundant physical charms and about the way she entered a room and the way she handled a knife and fork, and I decided to make an effort.

I went about it, as in all things, systematically. I gave her a course in logic. It happened that I, as a law student, was taking a course in logic myself, so I had all the facts at my fingertips. "Polly," I said to her when I picked her up on the next date, "tonight we are going over to the Knoll and talk."

"Oo, terrif," she replied. One thing I will say for this girl: you would go far to find another so agreeable.

We went to the Knoll, the campus trysting place, and we sat down under an old oak, and she looked at me expectantly. "What are we going to talk about?" she asked.

"Logic."

She thought this over for a minute and decided she liked it. "Magnif," she said.

"Logic," I said, clearing my throat, "is the science of thinking. Before we can think correctly, we must first learn to recognize the common fallacies of logic. These we will take up tonight."

"Wow-dow!" she cried, clapping her hands delightedly.

I winced, but went bravely on. "First let us examine the fallacy called Dicto Simpliciter."

"By all means," she urged, batting her lashes eagerly.

"Dicto Simpliciter means an argument based on an unqualified generalization. For example: Exercise is good. Therefore, everybody should exercise."

"I agree," said Polly earnestly. "I mean exercise is wonderful. I mean it builds the body and everything."

"Polly," I said gently, "the argument is a fallacy. Exercise is good is an unqualified generalization. For instance, if you have heart disease, exercise is bad, not good. Many people are ordered by their doctors not to exercise. You must qualify the generalization. You must say exercise is usually good, or exercise is good for most people. Otherwise you have committed a Dicto Simpliciter. Do you see?"

"No." she confessed. "But this is marvy. Do more! Do more!"

"It will be better if you stop tugging at my sleeve," I told her, and when she desisted, I continued. "Next we take up a fallacy called Hasty Generalization.

Listen carefully: You can't speak French. I can't speak French. Petey Burch can't speak French. I must therefore conclude that nobody at the University of Minnesota can speak French."

"Really?" said Polly, amazed. "Nobody?"

I hid my exasperation. "Polly, it's a fallacy. The generalization is reached too hastily. There are too few instances to support such a conclusion."

"Know any more fallacies?" she asked breathlessly. "This is more fun than dancing even."

I fought off a wave of despair. I was getting nowhere with this girl, absolutely nowhere. Still, I am nothing if not persistent. I continued. "Next comes Post Hoc. Listen to this: Let's not take Bill on our picnic. Every time we take him out with us, it rains."

"I know somebody just like that," she exclaimed. "A girl back home – Eula Becker, her name is. It never fails. Every single time we take her on a picnic–"

"Polly," I said sharply, "It's a fallacy. Eula Becker doesn't cause the rain. She has no connection with the rain. You are guilty of Post Hoc if you blame Eula Becker."

"I'll never do it again," she promised contritely. "Are you mad at me?"

I sighed deeply. "No, Polly, I'm not mad."

"Then tell me some more fallacies."

"All right. Let's try Contradictory Premises."

"Yes, let's," she chirped, blinking her eyes happily.

I frowned, but plunged ahead. "Here's an example of Contradictory Premises: If God can do anything, can He make a stone so heavy that He won't be able to lift it?"

"Of course," she replied promptly.

"But if He can do anything, He can lift the stone," I pointed out.

"Yeah," she said thoughtfully. "Well, then I guess He can't make the stone."

"But He can do anything," I reminded her.

She scratched her pretty, empty head. "I'm all confused," she admitted.

"Of course you are. Because when the premises of an argument contradict each other, there can be no argument. If there is an irresistible force, there can be no immovable object. If there is an immovable object, there can be no irresistible force. Get it?"

"Tell me some more of this keen stuff," she said eagerly.

I consulted my watch. "I think we'd better call it a night. I'll take you home now, and you go over all the things you've learned. We'll have another session tomorrow night."

I deposited her at the girls' dormitory, where she assured me that she had had a perfectly terrif evening, and I went glumly home to my room. Petey lay snoring in his bed, the raccoon coat huddled like a great hairy beast at his feet. For a moment I considered waking him and telling him that he could have his girl back. It seemed clear that my project was doomed to failure. The girl simply had a logic-proof head.

But then I reconsidered. I had wasted one evening; I might as well waste another. Who knew? Maybe somewhere in the extinct crater of her mind, a few embers still smoldered. Maybe somehow I could fan them into flame. Admittedly it was not a prospect fraught with hope, but I decided to give it one more try.

Seated under the oak the next evening I said, "Our first fallacy tonight is called Ad Misericordiam."

She quivered with delight.

"Listen closely," I said. "A man applies for a job. When the boss asks him what his qualifications are, he replies that he has a wife and six children at home, the wife is a helpless cripple, the children have nothing to eat, no clothes to wear, no shoes on their feet, there are no beds in the house, no coal in the cellar, and winter is coming."

A tear rolled down each of Polly's pink cheeks. "Oh, this is awful, awful," she sobbed.

"Yes, it's awful," I agreed, "but it's no argument. The man never answered the boss's question about his qualifications. Instead he appealed to the boss's sympathy. He committed the fallacy of Ad Misericordiam. Do you understand?"

"Have you got a handkerchief?" she blubbered.

I handed her a handkerchief and tried to keep from screaming while she wiped her eyes. "Next," I said in a carefully controlled tone, "we will discuss False Analogy. Here is an example: Students should be allowed to look at their textbooks during examinations. After all, surgeons have X-rays to guide them during an operation, lawyers have briefs to guide them during a trial, carpenters have blueprints to guide them when they are building a house. Why, then, shouldn't students be allowed to look at their textbooks during an examination?"

"There now," she said enthusiastically, "is the most marvy idea I've heard in years."

"Polly," I said testily, "the argument is all wrong. Doctors, lawyers, and carpenters aren't taking a test to see how much they have learned, but students are. The situations are altogether different, and you can't make an analogy between them."

"I still think it's a good idea," said Polly.

"Nuts," I muttered. Doggedly I pressed on. "Next we'll try Hypothesis Contrary to Fact."

"Sounds yummy," was Polly's reaction. "Listen: If Madame Curie had not happened to leave a photographic plate in a drawer with a chunk of pitchblende, the world today would not know about radium."

"True, true," said Polly, nodding her head. "Did you see the movie? Oh, it just knocked me out. That Walter Pidgeon is so dreamy. I mean he fractures me."

"If you can forget Mr Pidgeon for a moment," I said coldly. "I would like to point out that the statement is a fallacy. Maybe Madame Curie would have discovered radium at some later date. Maybe somebody else would have discovered it. Maybe any number of things would have happened. You can't start with a hypothesis that is not true and then draw any supportable conclusions from it."

"They ought to put Walter Pidgeon in more pictures," said Polly. "I hardly ever see him anymore."

One more chance, I decided. But just one more. There is a limit to what flesh and blood can bear. "The next fallacy is called Poisoning the Well."

"How cute!" she gurgled.

"Two men are having a debate. The first one gets up and says, 'My opponent is a notorious liar. You can't believe a word that he is going to say'... Now, Polly, think. Think hard. What's wrong?"

I watched her closely as she knit her creamy brow in concentration. Suddenly a glimmer of intelligence – the first I had seen – came into her eyes. "It's not fair," she said with indignation. "It's not a bit fair. What chance has the second man got if the first man calls him a liar before he even begins talking?"

"Right!" I cried exultantly. "One hundred percent right. It's not fair. The first man has poisoned the well before anybody could drink from it. He has hamstrung his opponent before he could even start... Polly I'm proud of you."

"Pshaw," she murmured, blushing with pleasure.

"You see, my dear, these things aren't so hard. All you have to do is concentrate. Think – examine – evaluate. Come now, let's review everything we have learned."

"Fire away," she said with an airy wave of her hand.

Heartened by the knowledge that Polly was not altogether a cretin, I began a long, patient review of all I had told her. Over and over and over again I cited instances, pointed out flaws, kept hammering away without let up. It was like digging a tunnel. At first everything was work, sweat, and darkness. I had no idea when I would reach the light, or even if I would. But I persisted. I pounded and clawed and scraped, and finally I was rewarded. I saw a chink of light. And then the chink got bigger and the sun came pouring in and all was bright.

Five grueling nights this took, but it was worth it. I had made a logician out of Polly; I had taught her to think. My job was done. She was worthy of me at last. She was a fit wife for me, a proper hostess for my many mansions, a suitable mother for my well-heeled children.

It must not be thought that I was without love for this girl. Quite the contrary. Just as Pygmalion loved the perfect woman he had fashioned, so I loved mine. I determined to acquaint her with my feelings at our very next meeting. The time had come to change our relationship from academic to romantic.

"Polly," I said when next we sat beneath our oak, "tonight we will not discuss fallacies."

"Aw, gee," she said, disappointed.

"My dear," I said, favoring her with a smile, "we have now spent five evenings together. We have gotten along splendidly. It is clear that we are well matched."

"Hasty Generalization," said Polly brightly.

"I beg your pardon," said I.

"Hasty Generalization," she repeated. "How can you say that we are well matched on the basis of only five dates?"

I chuckled with amusement. The dear child had learned her lessons well. "My dear," I said, patting her hand in a tolerant manner, "five dates is plenty. After all, you don't have to eat a whole cake to know that it's good."

"False Analogy," said Polly promptly. "I'm not a cake. I'm a girl."

I chuckled with somewhat less amusement. The dear child had learned her lessons perhaps too well. I decided to change tactics. Obviously the best approach was a simple, strong, direct declaration of love. I paused for a moment while my massive brain chose the proper words. Then I began:

"Polly, I love you. You are the whole world to me, and the moon, and the stars and the constellations of outer space. Please, my darling, say that you will go steady with me, for if you will not, life will be meaningless. I will languish. I will refuse my meals. I will wander the face of the earth, a shambling, hollow-eyed hulk."

There, I thought, folding my arms, that ought to do it.

"Ad Misericordiam," said Polly.

I ground my teeth. I was not Pygmalion; I was Frankenstein, and my monster had me by the throat. Frantically I fought back the tide of panic surging through me. At all costs I had to keep cool.

"Well, Polly," I said, forcing a smile, "you certainly have learned your fallacies."

"You're darn right," she said with a vigorous nod.

"And who taught them to you, Polly?"

"You did."

"That's right. So you do owe me something, don't you, my dear? If I hadn't come along you never would have learned about fallacies."

"Hypothesis Contrary to Fact," she said instantly.

I dashed perspiration from my brow. "Polly," I croaked, "you mustn't take all these things so literally. I mean this is just classroom stuff. You know that things you learn in school don't have anything to do with life."

"Dicto Simpliciter," she said, wagging her finger at me playfully. That did it. I leaped to my feet, bellowing like a bull. "Will you or will you not go steady with me?"

"I will not," she replied.

"Why not?" I demanded.

"Because this afternoon I promised Petey Burch that I would go steady with him."

I reeled back, overcome with the infamy of it. After he promised, after he made a deal, after he shook my hand! "The rat!" I shrieked, kicking up great chunks of turf. "You can't go with him, Polly. He's a liar. He's a cheat. He's a rat."

"Poisoning the Well" said Polly, "and stop shouting. I think shouting must be a fallacy too."

With an immense effort of will, I modulated my voice. "All right," I said. "You're a logician. Let's look at this thing logically. How could you choose Petey Burch over me? Look at me – a brilliant student, a tremendous intellectual, a man with an assured future. Look at Pete – a knothead, a jitterbug, a guy who'll never know where his next meal is coming from. Can you give me one logical reason why you should go steady with Petey Burch?"

"I certainly can," declared Polly. "He's got a raccoon coat."

Reading questions 7.a

1. This story's humor is based, in part, on the error of "hasty generalization" – "jumping to a conclusion" that is not based on facts and research. What generalization does the narrator (the "I" of the story) make about Polly Espy that turns out not to be true?

2. The end of this story reminds us to respect "matters of taste." Explain how the narrator attempts to "prove" a point that is actually a matter of taste, and is not appropriately open to a line of reasoning.

3. Go back through the story and list the fallacies that the narrator teaches Polly. Review these fallacies and identify each one as a fallacy in processing information or a fallacy about people and personalities. Use the answers *Process Fallacy* and *Personality Fallacy* to simplify your responses.

Persuasion in Poetry

During the Elizabethan era, a well-known poet, Christopher Marlow, wrote this poem in the voice of a young man, hoping to persuade a young lady (his "nymph") to go along with his plan. Later, a friend of Marlowe's, the famous Sir Walter Raleigh (another Renaissance man) wrote an "answer" to Marlowe in the voice of the young lady. This "conversation" has gone down in literary history as one of the most famous debates to take place on the literary page. As you read the two poems, evaluate each narrator's expertise in argument.

The Passionate Shepherd to His Love
by Christopher Marlowe (1564–1593)

Come live with me and be my love,
And we will all the pleasures prove
That valleys, groves, hills, and fields,
Woods, or steepy mountain yields.

And we will sit upon the rocks,
Seeing the shepherds feed their flocks,
By shallow rivers to whose falls
Melodious birds sing madrigals.

And I will make thee beds of roses
And a thousand fragrant posies,
A cap of flowers, and a kirtle
Embroidered all with leaves of myrtle;

A gown made of the finest wool
Which from our pretty lambs we pull;
Fair lined slippers for the cold,
With buckles of the purest gold;

A belt of straw and ivy buds,
With coral clasps and amber studs:
And if these pleasures may thee move,
Come live with me, and be my love.

The shepherds' swains shall dance and sing
For thy delight each May morning:
If these delights thy mind may move,
Then live with me and be my love.

Reading questions 7.b

1. What is the shepherd asking the "nymph"? What is noticeably absent from his request?

2. What type of "evidence" does he provide to show that his idea is worthwhile?

3. Do you think he is convincing? What will her answer be?

Now, read the young lady's reply:

The Nymph's Reply to the Shepherd
by Sir Walter Raleigh (1522(?)–1618)

If all the world and love were young,
And truth in every shepherd's tongue,
These pretty pleasures might me move
To live with thee and be thy love.

Time drives the flocks from field to fold
When rivers rage and rocks grow cold,
And Philomel becometh dumb;
The rest complains of cares to come.

The flowers do fade, and wanton fields
To wayward winter reckoning yields;
A honey tongue, a heart of gall,
Is fancy's spring, but sorrow's fall,

Thy gowns, thy shoes, thy beds of roses,
Thy cap, thy kirtle, and thy posies
Soon break, soon wither, soon forgotten –
In folly ripe, in reason rotten.

Thy belt of straw and ivy buds,
Thy coral clasps and amber studs,
All these in me no means can move
To come to thee and be thy love.

> But could youth last and love still breed,
> Had joys no date nor age no need,
> Then these delights my mind may move
> To live with thee and be thy love.

Reading questions 7.c

1. Sum up her answer in a word: does she say yes or no? What other observations can you make about her response?
2. The nymph uses an analogy in her line of reasoning. Explain her use of the seasons to make an analogy about life. Use the two analogy criteria presented in Chapter 4 to evaluate her analogy of the seasons.

The next two poems are classic pieces that also make use of metaphor as a literary device and analogy as an argument to convince. As the analogy in each poem unfolds, we see why analogy is such an effective form of persuasion. The Renaissance man was proud of his thinking skills and his ability to use lyrical voice for pathos to enhance his powers of persuasion.

This poem by Robert Herrick is short, and quickly gets to the point:

To the Virgins, to Make Much of Time
by Robert Herrick (1591–1674)

> Gather ye rosebuds while ye may,
>   Old Time is still a-flying;
> And this same flower that smiles today
>   Tomorrow will be dying.
>
> The glorious lamp of heaven, the sun,
>   The higher he's a-getting,
> The sooner will his race be run,
>   And nearer he's to setting.
>
> That age is best which is the first,
>   When youth and blood are warmer;
> But being spent, the worse, and worst
>   Times still succeed the former.

> Then be not coy, but use your time,
>   And while ye may, go merry;
> For having lost but once your prime,
>   You may forever tarry.

Reading questions 7.d

1. As noted above, this poet has given his narrator the use of analogy. Explain the analogy and discuss how the use of figurative language increases the effectiveness of the poem.

2. Will the young lady to whom the poem is addressed be convinced?

This next selection by Andrew Marvell is longer, but continues the use of the same theme and a similar use of analogy, especially at the end. The language is a little stronger than Herrick's more light-hearted banter. Read closely to determine what part of the analogy makes a stronger point.

To His Coy Mistress
by Andrew Marvell (1621–1678)

> Had we but world enough, and time,
> This coyness, Lady, were no crime.
> We would sit down and think which way
> To walk and pass our long love's day.
> Thou by the Indian Ganges' side
> Shouldst rubies find: I by the tide
> Of Humber would complain. I would
> Love you ten years before the Flood,
> And you should, if you please, refuse
> Till the conversion of the Jews.
> My vegetable love should grow
> Vaster than empires, and more slow;
> An hundred years should go to praise
> Thine eyes and on thy forehead gaze;
> Two hundred to adore each breast;
> But thirty thousand to the rest;
> An age at least to every part,
> And the last age should show your heart;
> For, Lady, you deserve this state,
> Nor would I love at lower rate.

But at my back I always hear
Time's wingèd chariot hurrying near;
And yonder all before us lie
Deserts of vast eternity.
Thy beauty shall no more be found,
Nor, in thy marble vault, shall sound
My echoing song: then worms shall try
That long preserved virginity,
And your quaint honour turn to dust,
And into ashes all my lust:
The grave's a fine and private place,
But none, I think, do there embrace.

Now therefore, while the youthful hue
Sits on thy skin like morning dew,
And while thy willing soul transpires
At every pore with instant fires,
Now let us sport us while we may,
And now, like amorous birds of prey,
Rather at once our time devour
Than languish in his slow-chapt power.
Let us roll all our strength and all
Our sweetness up into one ball,
And tear our pleasures with rough strife
Thorough the iron gates of life:
Thus, though we cannot make our sun
Stand still, yet we will make him run.

Reading questions 7.e

1. What similar metaphors and analogies does Marvell's poem use? What new items does he include? What added image does this narrator use to increase the power of his argument? Is this similar to the fallacy seen in Herrick's poem?

2. All of these poems use the seasons and the sun/heavens to create analogies. Why would this be effective?

These poems from the sixteenth and seventeenth centuries focus on a topic that is always current: young men and women falling in love. Look for examples in modern songs, television shows and cinema that demonstrate new versions of the age-old story of boy-meets-girl.

PUTTING IT ALL TOGETHER: A RESEARCH PROJECT

Now that you have studied the argument process, you can put your knowledge to work in a persuasive research project. To complete this project, we will follow the four steps outlined in Chapter 2, "How Does Argument Happen?":

1. Determine an arguable proposition.
2. Gather and evaluate the evidence needed to support a preferred side of the controversy.
3. Gather and evaluate evidence to understand the views of the opposition.

And finally…

4. Reason to a conclusion.

A persuasive research paper or report can be a daunting task. To complete it, we'll follow the popular answer to a challenging question: "How do you eat an elephant?" The answer: "One bite at a time!"

We will work through our research assignment step by step. At the end of this chapter is a checklist that will keep you focused.

Selecting a Topic and Forming a Proposition

In an academic social studies or writing class, a teacher might assign a topic for debate.

At work, a supervisor might give you the task of gathering data to support a new company initiative. In both cases, you can move forward and construct your presentation.

When you are assigned a topic in a classroom or given a project to review at work, the first step is solved for you – the topic is selected.

Sometimes, you are fortunate enough to select your own topic for research. You can work on a subject in which you already have an interest and about which you already have a point of view and perhaps even some background information. In this case, you have a different advantage: you like the topic at hand. Or, you may be given the freedom to pick a topic, but you aren't sure what you might be interested in.

To help you select a topic when the options are open, here is a list of current controversial topics that lend themselves to debate, and that fit a number of different courses of study. These topics may also be used in an academic setting where you are asked to complete a "multidisciplinary report," that is, a report that may be submitted to more than one instructor. You might write this paper for both a composition class and a sociology/history class if your instructors in both classes assign a multidisciplinary project.

In the interest of academic honesty, if the assignment is not presented by both instructors, tell each instructor that you would like to submit the project for both classes and get permission to do so.

Current topics for interdisciplinary research

Sciences and health/medicine:

- Political correctness and research funding
- The Gardasil controversy
- Organic food (good or bad?) and food/farming issues
- Doping/drugs: enhancement in athletics
- DNA information and health insurance coverage

Psychology:

- The homeless (diagnosis, commitment, insurance)
- Rewards and self-esteem
- The effects of divorce on children

Art:
- Funding "controversial" artists
- Requiring art/music classes in public schools

History/humanities:
- Jerusalem as an independent holy city
- Empowering the UN
- Diplomacy/cooperation on any issue
- Human trafficking vs. legalized prostitution
- Internet control/censorship in developing countries
- Permitting/not permitting soldiers to smoke
- Permitting/not permitting pregnant soldiers to serve in combat

Economics:
- Federal Reserve policy
- Small IPOs trading outside the US

Technology:
- Should professionals (teachers, nurses, doctors) have a Facebook page?
- Parental control on teenagers' computers
- Wisdom of making friends on social networking sites

Good topic choices for statistics classes:

Projects that are data-heavy, such as research concerns in the sciences and insurance issues that look at actuarial projections, correlate well with statistics classes. The challenge is to present the data along with a coherent explanation that promotes a proposition.

Good topic choices for English and writing classes:

Any of the projects listed above are appropriate for an English/writing class project that involves research, writing skills and critical thinking.

Getting started

To get started, select a topic and do some preliminary research. Preliminary research is easier than it sounds: it means to read several short current articles to raise your awareness on the current level of debate regarding the selected topic.

If you have an idea about where you stand, that is a fair way to start. In fact, you may want to do your early research looking for information that supports your point of view. Remember to stay flexible. Review the information on flexibility of thinking in Chapter 1. You need to be open to all the available information on the topic.

Example: You might be a student in Advanced Psychology, and you might be interested in pursuing the topic "The Effects of Divorce on Children." You might even have an established point of view – that it is better for children if the parents get divorced, rather than having them watch their parents argue. Or alternately, you might believe that divorce is devastating to children and should be avoided in most cases. Either way, there is a good chance that you already have a view based on experiences of people you know from everyday life. This is a good start. Just remember to keep an open mind, allow the research to develop, and evaluate the evidence that you find.

Remember the note in Chapter 2: before this project is finished, you may even change your mind!

The proposition and the thesis statement

As an experienced writer, you know that it is important to start with a **thesis statement**. This thesis becomes the focus of the paper. In a persuasive paper, the thesis is the **proposition**, or the statement to be argued. You learned the characteristics of a good proposition in Chapter 2. Once you have selected a topic, you should write a preliminary, or starting, proposition. This will clarify and narrow the goal of the research and the paper itself.

You can make changes in your proposition as you move through the research and reasoning phases of the project; you can edit and refine the proposition. And, unless you are assigned one side of the issue, as happens in a formal debate, you can change sides and write a proposition that supports your new focus. But to get started, it is important to start with a working proposition.

Review Chapter 2 to write a strong proposition that will become the focus of your paper.

Gathering, Evaluating and Organizing Evidence

In Chapter 3, we discussed gathering and evaluating evidence. Now that you have selected a topic for your persuasive paper, it is time to get to the serious work of researching your topic.

Start by doing some preliminary reading: You might see a newspaper or news magazine article on your topic. Even if you feel that you know your topic, read these preliminary articles with a fresh perspective: notice how the professional author presents and organizes information. Chapter 1 provides some practice in organization, with the reminder that organizing abstract ideas can be more difficult than organizing items. Learn from professional writers how to best subdivide the issues and organize the debate on your chosen subject.

Start a notebook: Take notes on the most important points in this early reading, and write down any questions that come to mind as you read.

Whether you are preparing a researched report for work or for an academic setting, you can do these starting activities at home.

Using the media center

After you complete the preliminary reading, it is time to move to the media center.

Introduce yourself to the librarian or "media specialist." Let this individual know your topic choice, and ask how to access the variety of sources available. You will probably need a code and a password to access the best databases. Remember the guidelines from Chapter 3: you want good, solid evidence from reliable sources.

The process of research

Researching is the most demanding part of writing a persuasive paper. Read, take notes, organize, and then repeat the process. Be thorough; as your read, take notes and label your notes and copies. Note how professional writers organize the divisions of the subject. In this way, the research itself helps you create an outline for your paper. Professional writers will bring up complex ideas – you will see where you must go back, look again and double check. Don't forget to **triangulate** (see Chapter 3) whenever you find conflicting evidence.

Writing and citing responsibly

Writing a research paper is not creative writing. The evidence you include in your paper will come from the investigations of many professionals. This is their daily work, and these professionals own their academic property. It is important that you acknowledge the sources of the information in your paper. Remember to cite responsibly, using the format (generally MLA or APA style) that is required by your instructor or employer, or that is most appropriate for your subject.

Keep a careful record of all bibliographical information, including authors, publishers, dates, pages and websites. Follow the correct forms and acknowledge (cite) all quotations, statistics and authoritative opinions and views.

Look for "issues"

The central point of your argument is the major premise, called the proposition, of your paper. It is the "thesis" of the entire debate. As you read, the minor premises, or issues, will emerge. You will see these as the "reasons" that support a particular side of the argument. Make a list of these "reasons" or "issues" as they appear when you read. These reasons/issues will become divisions in the outline of your paper and the paragraph points when you write the full text of the report.

Organize the evidence

In the early stages of reading, your "mental organizer" will start to see that professional writers who are dealing with your topic identify the issues and talk about them one at a time, giving evidence for each issue in an organized fashion. As you gather more and more evidence, organize your ideas along these same lines, creating a pen-and-paper outline for your paper.

In the following section, you will find two easy ways to outline the persuasive paper. Both formats include a basic guideline for an introduction, a background paragraph that gives your reader a basic history of your debate, followed by a sensible way to create a line of reasoning.

Understanding "pros and cons" in the outline process

We will need to define **pro** and **con** to create our outline. The **pro** position in an argument is the accumulation of information and reasons that support the proposition. The **con** refers to any information or reasoning that speaks against the proposition.

Notice that you must have a **proposition** before you can identify the **pros and cons**. Once you have written a proposition, you can **group your reasons** into pros and cons. If you change your mind, and move to the other side of the argument, you must write a new proposition that declares the new position you are taking. The **pros and cons** will now be reassigned so that the pro information supports the new declaration and the cons work against it.

Listing the pros and cons one at a time is a straightforward way to outline a persuasive paper. You provide all of the evidence that supports your side of the argument – the pros – and then acknowledge the other side's reasons – the cons – and then finish your argument by refuting the cons.

Writing Hint: When you write out the paper, each Roman numeral (see below) will correspond to a paragraph. If the paragraphs are large, make paragraph breaks at each lettered section.

PERSUASIVE OUTLINE FORM # 1:
The Pro and Con Outline

I. Introduction

    A. Attention getter (a short human-interest story or surprising statistic)

    B. Common ground (why everyone should care about this topic)

    C. The proposition (the thesis, or statement to be proven)

II. Background information

    A. General data (the number of people involved, the extent of the problem, etc.)

    B. How this controversy developed

    C. Why this controversy is important today

    D. Definitions (define all key words in the argument)

III. The pros (reasons on your side)

Here, you may want to make one full paragraph for each lettered reason or issue

    A. Reason or issue #1 (supply data and evidence in each lettered section)

    B. Reason or issue #2

C. Reason or issue #3

Continue as needed

IV. The cons (reasons given by the other side)

A. Reason or issue #1

B. Reason or issue #2

C. Reason or issue #3

Continue as needed

V. Rebuttal (refutation of the opposition)

Follow the lettered items from the "con" section and explain why their reasons are not as strong as your "pros"

VI. Conclusion

You may use the last paragraph to "reason" to your "conclusion"

Remember, your conclusion is a restatement of the proposition

Writing hints: The conclusion

1. The conclusion has a tone of finality.
2. No new information can be placed in the conclusion.
3. The conclusion restates the "thesis" (**proposition**) in wording that is similar to, but not exactly the same as, the wording used in the opening paragraph.
4. In a longer paper, you may need a two-part conclusion with a paragraph to present the final line of reasoning, and then a brief paragraph to emphasize and restate the proposition.

Working with issues as an alternate outline option

Next, we will look at an outline form that uses the **issues** to create subheadings in the outline format. The issues outline uses the same basic tenants of the pro/con outline. The only difference is that it deals with one issue at a time, revealing the pros and cons as further subdivisions of that category. If you need to review the concept of **issues**, return to Chapter 2. You will have to make a list of the issues for your topic before you can make this outline. This format is appropriate for a more complicated topic.

PERSUASIVE OUTLINE FORM #2:
The Issue Outline

I. Introduction

    A. Attention getter (a short human-interest story or surprising statistic)

    B. Common ground (why everyone should care about this topic)

    C. The proposition (the thesis, or statement to be proven)

II. Background information

    A. General data (the number of people involved, the extent of the problem, etc.)

    B. How this controversy developed

    C. Why this controversy is important today

    D. Definitions (define all key words in the argument)

III. Issue #1

    A. Data and evidence that supports your side

    B. Data/evidence on this issue provided by the opposition

    C. Rebuttal of the opposition's views

III. Issue #2

    A. Data and evidence that supports your side

    B. Data/evidence on this issue provided by the opposition

    C. Rebuttal of the opposition's views

III. Issue #3

    A. Data and evidence that supports your side

    B. Data/evidence on this issue provided by the opposition

    C. Rebuttal of the opposition's views

Add Roman numeral sections for additional issues

    V. Summation paragraph

        In this paragraph, you will make a brief summary of the pro portion of each issue, showing how, as they are gathered together, the pros make a strong case in support of the proposition

You may "reason" to your conclusion here, or in the conclusion paragraph itself

VI. Conclusion

You may use the last paragraph to "reason" to your "conclusion"

Remember, your conclusion is a restatement of the proposition – see "Writing Hints: The Conclusion" above

Returning to research

Your outline serves two purposes:

1. The outline organizes the information to help the reader process the argument.

2. The outline reveals where your research is incomplete.

If you haven't found information for any given section of your outline, go back to the media center and fill in the gaps. Here, especially, you will happy that you introduced yourself and your topic to the media specialist, who will be glad to help you follow through with your project and find the tough, challenging bits of data needed for the completion your paper.

Writing, Citing and Editing

A completed outline is the most important writing tool at your disposal. If you have completed the outline and returned to the library for any needed information, you are now ready to write.

Writing from your outline

Gather all the material you need to write the text of your paper; have your material handy at your computer. Along with the outline you created, you may want to have with you additional tools, such as a calculator, as well as some of your original research sources

Start with the introduction and work your way through the outline. Remember that a general rule of thumb is that each Roman numeral in the outline will become a paragraph. If the Roman numeral section is large, make paragraph divisions for each lettered section.

As you write, use transitions when you move from section to section. (If you need help with transitions, ask your writing teacher or go to an online site to review transition words and phrases.) Your skillful use of paragraph divisions and transitions will guide the reader through your line of reasoning and make your argument more convincing.

Citing as you write

Create your "Works Cited" or "References" document as a companion document that you keep open while you write the text of your paper. If you are working in a classroom setting, your teacher may have asked you to start this document on the same day that you started researching. Make sure that you include all the sources that provide quotations, statistics, charts and unusual ideas for your text.

In the text portion of the paper, create an in-text citation each time you include a quotation, data or statistics, charts, graphs, pictorials or any unusual opinions, even those that you paraphrase. Double-check each in-text citation to ascertain that the source is included on the "Works Cited"/"References" page.

Note: Research Responsibility. In a writing class or a research class, you may have had the opportunity to learn to cite your sources responsibly. Most writers use the MLA (Modern Language Association) or APA (American Psychiatric Association) formats to acknowledge sources. If you need to review these concepts, ask your teacher or go to an online site to learn the commonly accepted forms for giving credit to your sources.

Edit and complete the finished manuscript

Editing is a multistep process. Make sure that you follow all of the steps before you declare your research piece "done." Follow these steps to edit your paper:

1. Let your computer do the first edit. Run the spell check and grammar check features and repair common errors.

2. Next, print a copy of your paper and pick up a pencil. Read through the manuscript, looking for mistakes that the spell and grammar checks did not identify. Mark the repairs with a pencil by underlining the problem area in the text and handwriting a recommendation in the margin. This read-through gives you the opportunity to check for clarity and for any missed citations.

3. Give this pencil-marked copy to another reader. Giving the reviewer your marked copy will save this reader from marking problem areas that you have already identified. Ask this reader to use a pen so that you can readily identify the new edits.

4. Go back to the computer. Open your draft of the manuscript and proceed with the edited printout on your desk. Work your way through the paper and make all the necessary edits.

5. Run spell check and grammar check one more time to make sure that you didn't add an error while you were making repairs. Print out your newest copy and read it one more time. Hopefully, it is ready to submit. But in your last read, you may find additional errors. If so, make repairs one more time, and *voila*! You have created a research masterpiece.

Checklist for the Persuasive Research Paper

This checklist will keep you focused. Try to complete each step before starting the next. Step five is the critical point in the research for this paper. At step five, you will know that you have sufficient information to complete a paper that successfully supports the proposition.

1. Select a topic
2. Read two or three preliminary articles, taking brief notes.
3. Form a proposition. ★See Step 5.
4. Locate a variety of sources on the topic.
5. **Read each source carefully, take notes, highlight and make margin comments to focus the reading toward the goal of proving your point.**

Carefully record all bibliographical information as you read.

★At this point, you should feel confident that you can support your thesis. Later, at Step 8, you may want to get additional information to fill in weak areas. Also, this is the point where you should feel confident about which side of the debate you are on. If you decide to change sides, now is the time to reconstruct your proposition.

6. Review citation forms (MLA, APA or the format assigned to this project).
7. Create a rough outline, using one of the formats given in this chapter.
8. Fill in the outline with evidence (data, opinions from authorities, etc.) and look for gaps in research.
9. Go back to the media center for fill-in information.

10. Write a rough draft, following the outline. Include all citations and a "Works Cited" page.
11. Edit the draft: read it yourself, from beginning to end. Ask one person to peer-edit the paper.
12. Make edits and print a polished draft.

Evaluating the persuasive research paper

Evaluate your own work before you turn the paper into your instructor. Use the checklist above to see that you did not omit any important steps in the process of gathering research, organizing the ideas and writing the paper.

You or your instructor may use the **rubric** in Appendix 4 to evaluate the paper. A **rubric** is a scoring guide for written work and projects. When you have a rubric, you, as the student, can see the qualities that matter the most in completing a paper or a project. Read through the paper you have written and look for the qualities in the rubric. This way, if you see deficiencies, you can correct them before you hand in the paper. If you are completing a paper for the workplace, you can use this rubric to evaluate the work before you show your supervisor the final project.

In this rubric, the persuasive research paper is evaluated in two categories:

1. The text: How well did you formulate the argument? Is your argument convincing?
2. The format: Did you edit the paper for correct manuscript form? Did you follow correct citation style, both within the text and on the reference page at the end?

Chapter Review

Directions: Complete a persuasive research paper, following the process in Chapter 8. (Select a topic, research the topic, organize the evidence and then write the text.) Use Appendix 4 to evaluate the final paper.

All in a Day's Work

You have just finished a major academic project that involves reasoning and logic. Remember to use your new skills every day. You will be more convincing in "kitchen table" discussions. You will be able to get people to act on important matters – vote for your candidate or make a contribution to an important cause.

Most importantly, encourage people to debate responsibly: no arguing about matters of taste or verifiable facts, and when discussing a controversial subject, research, research, research!

APPENDIX 1

ANSWERS TO PRACTICE EXERCISES AND CHAPTER REVIEWS

Chapter 1 Practice Exercises

Practice 1.a

Answers will vary. Popular answers include evaluate, designate, hesitate, remediate and concentrate.

Practice 1.b

Answers will vary. Note that classmates will see similarities. Most students will also have strong opinions about what does not go in certain areas.

Practice 1.c

Answers will vary. Again, classmates will see similarities. Also, students will show strong opinions about what cannot be stored in certain areas. For example, we don't put glasses in drawers, or utensils on shelves.

Practice 1.d

Njym entz.

Practice 1.e

One answer: 2 quarters, 3 dimes and 20 pennies. There are other possible combinations.

Practice 1.f

Monday. One easy way to start solving this puzzle is to write the words "yesterday," "the day before yesterday" and "the day before the day before yesterday" in reverse order, like this:

> "the day before the day before yesterday" – "the day before yesterday" – "yesterday"
>
> Then, write the word "Tuesday" under "the day before the day before yesterday."

Fill in the next two weekdays under the word sequence, and then continue the sequence and you will see the answer.

Practice 1.g

Answers will vary. Whenever possible, students should share answers with another person to understand the similarities and differences in how people approach problem solving.

Chapter 2 Practice Exercises

Practice 2.a

1. GP.

2. NP. Reason: matter of taste. Cannot be rewritten to make a good proposition.

3. NP. Reason: two propositions written in one sentence. To edit, write two separate propositions.

4. NP. Reason: it is in question form. To edit, rewrite in declarative form: "The Supreme Court should reverse the *Roe v Wade* decision."

5. NP. Reason: matter of taste. Cannot be rewritten to make a good proposition.

6. NP. Verifiable fact.

7. NP. Contains biased wording. To edit, remove "inefficient."

8. GP.

9. GP.

10. NP. Contains biased wording. To edit, remove "irresponsible" and "precious."

Practice 2.b

Answers will vary. A current newspaper will provide any number of issues that are currently up for debate. Read the editorial page and "Letter to the Editor" sections for the most controversial subjects. The letters to the editor will give the best sense of both sides of a given controversy. Students should remember to credit their sources.

Practice 2.c

Students should first rewrite the question in a declarative sentence to form a proposition. Then, students should be able to identify three or more minor premises for each proposition.

Chapter 2 Review

1. Matters of taste, verifiable facts.

2. Act.

3. 1) Develop an arguable proposition. 2) Gather evidence to support the position. 3) Gather evidence to understand the opposition. 4) Reason to a conclusion.

4. Proposition.

5. Minor premise, issue.

6. 1) It is not about matters of taste or verifiable facts. 2) It is stated in a declarative sentence. 3) It contains no biased words. 4) It is clear, not ambiguous. 5) It is singular.

7. Item one is in the form of a question (characteristic #2).

    Item two is a matter of taste (characteristic #1).

    Item three is two propositions (characteristic #5).

    Item four is a verifiable fact (characteristic #1).

    Item five contains biased words (characteristic #3).

8. Items one, three and five can be repaired. Rewrites will vary slightly. These examples show improved propositions:

   "High school baseball teams should not use aluminum bats."

   "This poor proposition must be rewritten as two separate propositions."

   "Employees at The Snack Shoppe should be permitted to trade scheduled hours."

   "Employees at The Snack Shoppe should be given a 10¢ hourly raise."

   "Our school should use unweighted averages to select the valedictorian."

9. Answers will vary. When we watch a debate, we should recognize that each issue brought up in the course of the debate can be formed into a proposition and argued on its own merit, outside of the candidate debate format.

10. Answers will vary. Remember to check each proposition against the five characteristics of a strong proposition.

Chapter 3 Practice Exercises

Practice 3.a

Answers will vary. Remember to check the date of each source. Select sources that are current so the data is up to date and the authorities have made their comments apropos to what is happening now. This is also a good time to remind everyone to make a notation of the sources used to locate the answers, including those that are "practice."

Practice 3.b

Answers will vary. After finding one piece of information from each type of "dot" site, you may begin to see the differences in how these sites are set up. You may get a sense of which sites are more reliable than others.

Practice 3.c

Answers will vary. You may locate some information that supports capital punishment, and some information that supports those who oppose it. Keep in mind that, as you research, you can look purposefully for information that helps your side of a controversy. At the same time, a good arguer is always on the lookout for information used by the opposition. This gives us a better understanding of the topic.

Practice 3.d

Answers will vary. This practice encourages you to look deeper and double-check your information. These are two habits that make truly good researchers, detectives and investigative journalists.

Chapter 3 Review

1. Good evidence is verifiable or attested to by a reliable authority.
2. 1) Evidence can be too old. 2) Information can be incorrect. 3) Information may be correct but stated in a misleading way. 4) The voice of authority may be used inappropriately.
3. A **reliable authority** is a person who has specific knowledge in his or her field. A **reliable source** is a knowledgeable source used by journalists to provide information for news articles. An **expert witness** is a reliable authority who has been called to testify in a court proceeding.
4. The identity of a reliable authority, who may also be called a reliable source in a courtroom, is known to all. The identity of a reliable source in journalism is often kept confidential.
5. Stacking the deck, or card stacking.
6. .com, .org, .edu, .gov.
7. Answers will vary.
8. Triangulate.
9. Answers will vary.
10. Issues.

Chapter 4 Practice Exercises

Practice 4.a

1. Poor generalization. Reason: too few instances are used.
2. Good generalization.
3. Poor generalization. Reason: instances are not typical.

Chapter 4 Review

1. Generalization.

2. Inductive leap.

3. Hasty generalization or jumping to a conclusion.

4. 1) A fair number of instances must be investigated. 2) Instances must be typical. 3) Negative instances must be explained.

5. Analogy.

6. 1) Items compared must be alike in important respects. 2) Differences must be accounted for as being unimportant.

7. Enhance meaning, reason to a conclusion.

Chapter 5 Practice Exercises

Exercise 5.a

1. "Constellation" is the outer circle and "the Big Dipper" goes in the inner circle. Or, you may just indicate "the Big Dipper" as an X inside the larger circle.

2. Create three circles. The largest circle is "animals," the next inner circle is "striped animals," and smallest circle is "zebras." It is also correct to use only two circles, for "striped animals" and "zebras."

3. The larger circle is "boys"; the inner circle is "members of the team."

4. "Citizens" is the largest circle; "those who can vote" goes in the inner circle.

5. "Cheese" is the larger circle and "brie" is the inner circle.

6. Put "healthy drinks" in the larger circle and put "milk" in the inner circle. It is also correct to make three circles, with "drinks" in the largest circle, followed by "healthy drinks" in the next circle, and then "milk" in the smallest circle.

7. The larger circle is "things that die"; the inner circle is "kings."

8. Put "brave" in the larger circle and "deserve the fair" in the inner circle.

9. Like in number eight, "brave" is the large circle and "deserve the fair" is the inner circle.

   Both number eight and number nine present the same idea. The concept is that no one outside the group of brave people will "deserve the fair." This is why "brave" is the larger circle. The challenge in numbers eight and nine is to work with the language. Words like "only" and the more sophisticated "none but the" require us to hone our skills in precision of language.

10. The larger circle is "men devoted to their families." The inner circle is "good men." Number ten creates the biggest categorization challenge, as most readers want to reverse the size of the categories at first try. But "good men" is not the larger category, although it is natural to think so. More consideration will bring you to the realization that even some "bad men" are devoted to their families. This makes "men devoted to their families" the bigger circle.

Practice 5.b

1. Valid.
2. Valid.
3. Invalid. The larger circle in the diagram is "shows that start at 6:00 p.m." We don't know if "the show she is watching" fits into the inner circle of "evening news."
4. Valid.
5. Invalid. The larger circle is "things with ears." A smaller circle is "zebras." "People" fit into the larger circle, but not into the "zebra" circle.
6. Invalid. The larger circle is "photographers." "Professional photographers" is the inner circle. Mark can be in the larger circle, and not be in the inner circle.
7. Valid.
8. Valid.
9. Valid.
10. Invalid. The larger circle is "cereal," with bran in an inner circle. "What Mandy eats" fits in the larger circle, but does not necessarily fit in the inner circle.

Practice 5.c

1. Invalid. Do not affirm the consequence.
2. Valid. You can affirm the condition.

    Hint: Number two presents a challenge in identifying the condition and the consequence. The condition is "Anyone who can't learn from experience." The consequence is "is a fool."
3. Invalid. Do not affirm the consequence.
4. Invalid. Do not affirm the consequence.
5. Valid. You may affirm the condition. However, the conclusion is not true, because the major premise is not true. Labradors can be black, yellow or chocolate.
6. Invalid. Do not deny the condition.
7. Invalid. Do not affirm the consequence.
8. Valid. You may deny the consequence.
9. Valid. You may deny the consequence.
10. Valid. You may affirm the condition.

Practice 5.d

1. Invalid. Do not affirm the consequence.
2. Invalid. Do not affirm the consequence.
3. Valid. You may affirm the condition.
4. Invalid. Do not deny the condition.
5. Valid. You may deny the consequence.
6. Invalid. Do not affirm the consequence.
7. Valid. You may affirm the condition.
8. Invalid. Do not affirm the consequence.
9. Invalid. Do not affirm the consequence.
10. Invalid. Do not deny the condition.
11. Valid. You may deny the consequence.

Chapter 5 Review

1. Reasoning by classes.
2. Valid.
3. Venn diagram.
4. Syllogism.
5. Condition.
6. Consequence.
7. Correctly argued.
8. Valid.
9. Invalid. (The converse of an if/then is not necessarily true.)
10. **Rule 1: You can affirm the condition.** The result will be **valid**.

    Rule 2: You should not affirm the consequence. The result will be **invalid**.

    Rule 3: You should not deny the condition. The result will be **invalid**.

    Rule 4: You can deny the consequence. The result will be **valid**.

Chapter 6 Practice Exercises

Practice 6.a

1. Begging the question. (The word "dangerous" has been begged.)
2. Faulty dilemma. (Other things might happen, and there's no certainty that any driver will have a problem or that the town will be sued.)
3. Parade of horrors/slippery slope. This may be a good place to note that most individuals think that the "slippery slope" concern is a perfectly valid argument. It is a very popular manner of thinking, but it is not good sense.
4. Ignoring the question.
5. Hypothesis contrary to fact. (The town council may have proceeded with repairs even without a citizen complaint.)

Practice 6.b

1. Parade of horrors/slippery slope.
2. Equivocation.
3. Argumentum ad hominem.
4. Ad misericordiam.
5. Hypothesis contrary to fact.
6. Appeal to force.
7. Begging the question.
8. Faulty dilemma.
9. Hypothesis contrary to fact.
10. Tu quoque.

Chapter 7 Practice Exercises

Reading questions 7.a

1. In this discussion response, answers will vary. Most readers will see that the narrator makes several "hasty generalizations" – that a girl as pretty as Polly can't be intelligent, too, that Polly will like the narrator because he is knowledgeable about logic and that an intelligent girl wouldn't be attracted by a guy (like Petey) who makes a fashion statement. The narrator's hasty generalizations are based on stereotypes that are humorously proven wrong.

2. Answers will vary. Essentially, love is not logical. As noted in Chapter 2, we should not be putting our energy into arguing about matters of taste, including whom we find attractive!

3. The narrator teaches Polly the following fallacies: dicto simpliciter, hasty generalization, post hoc/propter hoc (just "Propter Hoc" in the story), contradictory premises, ad misericordiam, false analogy, hypothesis contrary to fact, and ad hominem (called "Poisoning the Well" in this story). Polly responds with dicto simpliciter, hasty generalization, ad misericordiam, false analogy, hypothesis contrary to fact and ad hominem. And Polly may be right – shouting should probably be a fallacy, too. Shouting makes people feel uncomfortable; it is the appeal to force fallacy. Reread the introduction to Chapter 1 for a review about what argument should and should not be.

Reading questions 7.b

1. The speaker, the young shepherd, is suggesting a romantic relationship to his lady friend. Students who are astute about the importance of definition (see "Equivocation" and "Note on Definition" in Chapter 6) will note that he is not offering marriage.

2. He offers a long list of tempting gifts, not reasons.

3. Answers will vary. Clearly, the shepherd is confident that the answer will be yes. Since we cannot hear the voice of the young lady, we can't be sure what she will say.

Reading Questions 7.c

1. The young lady says no. She starts her response with a humorous take on poisoning the well: if there were "truth in every shepherd's tongue," she might think about it, but she is clearly not convinced that this relationship would be a good idea.

2. The young lady responds by making an analogy to the seasons. She starts by saying that the shepherd's offer is like summer – full of "pretty pleasures" – but that the summer season will turn to fall and winter when "flowers do fade." She makes a thorough analogy, suggesting that his love, like the seasons, may turn cold, especially as she gets older and enters the "winter" of her years.

3. This is a poem, and the poet uses figurative language, the metaphor, to enhance the effect of his work. But the "logic" behind the lady's answer is the analogy process. See the section on "The Analogy" in Chapter 4 to review analogy, simile and metaphor. The analogy holds up pretty well because the seasons, like human lives, move onward, and it is wise to prepare for both the literal and figurative winters in our lives.

Reading questions 7.d

1. In this poem, the analogy and the metaphor are closely entwined. Like Marlow and Raleigh, Herrick uses his skill in lyrical language, using the metaphor and other figurative language to promote his "argument." Here, love is compared to a flower, and life to the course of the sun. In both cases, the narrator reminds his lover that the flower will fade and the sun will keep moving across the sky. He is hoping his young lady will agree to enjoy his attentions now, before it is too late.

2. The fallacy is appeal to force. There is a veiled threat, implying that if the young lady does not say yes now, she may find herself alone and sorry in the future.

Reading questions 7.e

1. Marvell includes references to flowers, all growing things – "my vegetable love" – and the sun. He adds a comparison to long walks, long adventures and classical stories to talk about how patient he would be if there was enough time. Finally, instead of suggesting to his lover that she will some day be old, he goes to the obvious conclusion and notes that she will eventually be dead, and that there will be no more opportunity for romance then! "The grave's a fine and private place / But none, I think, do there embrace."

2. The Renaissance was a time of renewed interest in science, including intense observation of the patterns of nature and the solar system. It's no surprise that the Renaissance man – who saw himself as poet, scientist and explorer – included references to the physical world in lyrical work.

Chapter 8 Review

Use the Persuasive Research Paper Rubric in Appendix 4 to evaluate your paper. The points awarded total 150.

Letter grade conversion:

> 135 to 150 points = A
>
> 120 to 134 points = B
>
> 105 to 133 points = C
>
> 90 to 104 points = D
>
> Below 90 points: Paper does not successfully complete the assignment.

Remember that the penalty for plagiarism at most schools and universities is high: a plagiarized paper does not pass. Always do your own work and cite properly.

APPENDIX 2

LOGIC TEST

Directions: Read through each question carefully. Write your answers on a separate answer sheet. When you are finished, check your answers against the answer key provided in Appendix 3.

1. True or false? "Valid" means "true."

2 and 3. Two types of reasoning are _____ and _____.

4 and 5. A sensible person does not argue about _____ or _____.

6. True or false? It is acceptable to put two issues in a proposition if the argument is carefully formulated.

7. A minor proposition that must be proven to support the main proposition is called _____.

8 and 9. Good evidence is either _____ or attested to by a _____.

Fill in these blanks to identify the three tests for generalization:

10. A fair number of _____ must be _____.

11. The instances must be _____.

12. _____ instances must be _____.

13. An opinion given by an authority is often called an _____.

14. The mental move from "some" to "all" is called the _____.

15 and 16. When reasoning by "either/or," two conditions must be met for validity. The two possibilities must be _____ and _____.

17. _____ means that the two possibilities must exist separately from each other.

18. _____ means that there may only be two possibilities.

19 and 20. The two tests for validity in an analogy are _____ and _____.

Questions 21 to 28. Draw a Venn diagram for each example. For 23 and 28 state whether the conclusion is valid or invalid.

21. The kangaroo is a marsupial.

22. Marsupials are mammals.

    The duck-billed platypus is a marsupial.

    ∴ The duck-billed platypus is a mammal.

23. The conclusion to number 22 is (valid /invalid).

24. The gazelle is a member of the antelope family of mammals.

25. All judges are lawyers.

26. Even teachers make mistakes.

27. All successful executives are intelligent men.

    Mr Baxter is an intelligent man.

    ∴ Mr Baxter is a successful executive.

28. The conclusion to number 27 is (valid / invalid).

Questions 29 to 33. Evaluate the following syllogisms. Tell whether the conclusion is valid or invalid. Then give the reason for your evaluation. Use these choices for your evaluation:

Valid: One may affirm the condition.

Valid: One may deny the consequence.

Invalid: One should not affirm the consequence.

Invalid: One should not deny the condition.

APPENDIX 2

29 and 30. The murderer was in Detroit on the night of the murder.

Spike was in Detroit the night of the murder.

∴ Spike is the murderer.

Valid or invalid? Reason?

31 and 32. All oak trees are deciduous.

That tree is not deciduous.

∴ That tree is not an oak.

Valid or invalid? Reason?

33 and 34. All residents are eligible to vote in this election.

Mr. Smith is a resident.

∴ Mr Smith is eligible to vote in this election.

Valid or invalid? Reason?

35 and 36. All West Point graduates are officers in the US Army.

Jones is an officer in the US Army.

∴ Jones is a graduate of West Point.

Valid or invalid? Reason?

37 and 38. The Native American respects his ancestor's culture.

That man respects his ancestor's culture.

∴ That man is a Native American.

Valid or invalid? Reason?

39 and 40. All As have some characteristics of Bs.

Item number six is an A.

∴ Item number six has some B characteristics.

Valid or invalid? Reason?

41 and 42. Deltas belong in the Alpha group.

Specimen A is not a Delta.

∴ Specimen A is also not an Alpha.

Valid or invalid? Reason?

Questions 43 to 50. **The following examples all contain errors in reasoning. Identify the major error in each example. Select your answer from this short list of fallacies. Each item in the list is used once.**

Begging the question	Ignoring the question
Dicto simpliciter	Faulty dilemma
Ad misericordiam	Argumentum ad hominem
Equivocation	Fallacy of composition/division

43. Some endangered species are rapidly disappearing. That animal running away from us is disappearing. It must be an endangered species.

44. The Army is notoriously inefficient. Sgt Jones is in the Army, so he must be very inefficient.

45. It is time to do something about the unhealthy lunches served in our school cafeteria.

46. Mr Lease suggested that Mrs Smith should not run for a New York senate seat because she is not a full-time resident. Well, I say, look at her record on education and childcare!

47. We all know that running is excellent exercise. Everyone should start running for better health.

48. So you want to go the party Friday night. Well, it's your choice! You can either go to the party and fail all of your classes, or stay home and get better grades.

49. Members of the Jury: As you begin your deliberations, I ask you to remember that my client is the sole support of his elderly parents. If he goes to jail, there will be no one to support them, no one to look after them, no one to comfort them in their old age. They face a bleak future if you find my client guilty!

50. Don't believe a thing my neighbor tells you! She is a nasty, cranky, irritable old gossip, and she's been impossible to get along with all the years we've lived next door.

APPENDIX 3

ANSWERS TO LOGIC TEST

1. False.
2. Inductive.
3. Deductive.
4. Verifiable facts.
5. Matters of taste.
6. False.
7. Issue.
8. Verifiable.
9. Reliable authority.
10. Instances, investigated.
11. Typical.
12. Atypical, explained as unimportant.
13. Educated guess.
14. Inductive leap.
15. Exclusive (or exhaustive).
16. Exhaustive (or exclusive).
17. Exclusive.
18. Exhaustive.
19. Alike in important respects.

20. Differences are accounted for as unimportant.

21. Larger circle is identified as "marsupials"; inner circle is "kangaroos." Alternately, a circle identified as "marsupials" with the word "kangaroos" outside the circle with an arrow pointing into the circle.

22. Largest circle is "mammals." Next inner circle is "marsupials." Smallest inner circle is "duck-billed platypus" or "the duck-billed platypus" outside two circles, with an arrow pointing into "marsupials."

23. Valid.

24. Largest circle is "mammals." Next inner circle is "antelopes." Smallest circle is "gazelles," or "the duck billed platypus" outside the circle, with the arrow pointing into "antelopes."

25. Outer circle is "lawyers." Inner circle is "judges."

26. Outer circle is "make mistakes." (Some students will write "people who make mistakes" in the larger circle.) Inner circle is "teachers."

27. Larger circle is "intelligent men." Inner circle is "successful businessmen." The words "Mr Baxter" should be written outside the circle set, with two arrows drawn. One arrow goes all the way in to "successful businessmen." The other arrow goes only in to the "intelligent men" circle. A question mark sits between the two arrows, indicating that we cannot tell where Mr Baxter fits in the diagram. Therefore, the answer to the next question (number 28) is…

28. Invalid.

29. Invalid.

30. One should not affirm the consequence.

31. Valid.

32. One may deny the consequence.

33. Valid.

34. One may affirm the condition.

35. Invalid.

36. One should not affirm the consequence.

37. Invalid.

38. One should not affirm the consequence.

39. Valid.
40. One may affirm the condition.
41. Invalid.
42. One should not deny the condition.
43. Equivocation.
44. Fallacy of composition/division.
45. Begging the question.
46. Ignoring the question.
47. Dicto simpliciter.
48. Faulty dilemma.
49. Ad misericordiam.
50. Argumentum ad hominem.

APPENDIX 4
Pursuasive Research Paper Rubric

CONTENT ___ out of 100 points

Research is thorough   20 points

    Information is complete
    Information is correct

Structure is appropriate
to debate process   20 points

    Opening paragraph:
        Attention getter
        Common ground
        Proposition worded correctly
    Body:
        Background
        Pros/cons
        Rebuttal
    Conclusion:
        No new information
        Reaffirms the proposition
        Tone of finality

**Organization supports
debate process   20 points**

    Outline available upon request
    Coherence: ideas presented in a
        logical order that aids the
        reader
    Emphasis: order of ideas
        promotes the writer's position
    Transitional words and phrases
        used effectively

FORMAT ___ out of 50 points

**Paper is clean, neat,
stapled   5 points**

**Format is correct
and complete   5 points**

MLA or APA
Heading or title page
Text with citations
Works Cited/References page
Outline available upon request

**Manuscript forms
are correct   15 points**

Citation forms/Works Cited/
    References
Margins, spacings, data, numbers
★Paraphrasing technique is at college
    level

Paper is edited   10 points

Spelling, mechanics
Grammar and diction
Syntax: sentence sense

Unity within paragraphs and
throughout paper
Sources are integrated

**Content successfully
completes argument   20 points**

Understanding of assignment
Proposition clear, single,
arguable
Thoroughly explores the issues
Details support writer's
position
Information attributed
correctly

Readability   20 points

Ideas flow clearly and sensibly
Sentence structure and
vocabulary are at college level
Student can deal with complex
ideas and technical information

**Research process
is evident   10 points**

Instructor has seen research
efforts, including sources and class
practices
Paper is responsibly researched

**Format concerns specific to this
paper to this paper   5 points**

*****Plagiarism will lower both content and format grades*****

INDEX

A

affirmation (in syllogisms) 48–55, 56
   affirming the condition 48–50
   affirming the consequence
      48–50, 56
ad hominem (fallacy) 68–9
ad misericordiam (fallacy) 69, 82, 85
ad populum (fallacy) 69
ad verecundiam (fallacy) 69–70
ambiguity 14–15
analogy 33–5, 82–3, 85
   false 82, 85
   practice for 34, 89–91
American Psychological Association
   (APA) 22, 98, 103, 104
Annie 35
appeal to force (fallacy) 69
appeal to pity (fallacy) 69
appeal to popular opinion
   (fallacy) 69
argument (defined) 9–12
argumentum ad hominem (fallacy)
   see ad hominem (fallacy)
Aristotle 2, 73, 75
authority 24, 27–8, 69–70
   appeal to 69–70
   by success 27
   by testimonial 27
   by transference 27
   voice of 27, 70
   see also ad verecundiam
      (fallacy)

B

bad evidence 25–7
bandwagon 69
begging the question (fallacy) 62–4
biased source *see* reliable source; card
   stacking
biased wording 14
   see also begging the question (fallacy)
bibliographical information 98, 104
   see also citation

C

capital punishment example 17–19,
   29–30
card stacking 23
Carroll, Lewis 52–3, 55
cause and effect 1, 65–6, 67
   see also post hoc
Christie, Agatha 64
circular argument 63
   see also begging the question (fallacy)
citation 21–2, 25, 29, 98, 103, 104–5
claims 75
classification 37–41
   practice 38–40
   see also Venn diagrams
.com *see* domains (network)
common sense 45, 49, 50, 52
comparison *see* analogy
composition and division (fallacies) 67
Conan Doyle, Arthur 64

conclusion 8, 11, 12, 31, 33, 39–40, 46–7, 49–51, 57, 66, 81, 83
  jumping to *see* hasty generalization (fallacy)
  in a research paper 100, 102
  in syllogisms 46–7, 49–51
condition 48–50, 53, 56, 58
  see also affirmation
consequence (in syllogisms) 48–50, 53–4, 56
critical thinking 1, 5, 8, 11, 40, 95

D

debate 2, 6, 9, 11–15, 18–22, 24–5, 28, 63, 65, 73–5, 83, 87, 93–4, 96–8, 104, 106
declarative sentence see proposition
deduction (deductive reasoning) 31, 37, 39–41, 43–7, 50, 56, 62, 73
definition of terms 65, 99, 101
"delving" 30
denial (in syllogisms) 48–51
  denying the condition 50
  denying the consequence 50
Department of Vital Statistics 24
determining validity practice 51–2
dicto simpliciter (fallacy) 66, 80, 85
division (fallacy) *see* composition and division (fallacies)
Dodgson, Charles L. *see* Carroll, Lewis
domains (network) 23, 29

E

earmarks 14, 16
.edu *see* domains (network)
either/or reasoning 56–8, 67
equivocation 64–5
ethos 73–5
everyman 69
evidence 11, 21–5, 27–9, 31, 45, 47, 66–7, 69, 88, 93, 96, 97–9, 101, 104
  evaluating 21, 23–5, 93, 96, 97
  gathering 21–2, 29, 93, 97
  organizing 28, 97–9, 101, 104
exclusive 56–7
exhaustive 56–7, 67

expert witness 24, 28
  see also authority
eyewitness 24

F

fallacies
  of people and personalities 68–71, 73
  of process 62–68
  practice with 68, 70–1
false analogy (fallacy) 82, 85
faulty dilemma (fallacy) 57, 67
figurative language 35, 90
flexibility with language 3–4, 96
force *see* appeal to force (fallacy)
four-step argument format 11, 93

G

generalization 31–2, 35, 37, 46, 66, 80–1, 86
  hasty *see* hasty generalization (fallacy)
  tests for 32, 35
  unqualified 66, 80
  see also dicto simpliciter (fallacy)
"Give me Liberty" (Henry) 74
.gov *see* domains (network)
grammar, rules of 32
grounds 75

H

hasty generalization (fallacy) 32, 62, 80, 84, 86
Henry, Patrick 73–4
Herrick, Richard 89, 90, 91
hypothesis contrary to fact (fallacy) 66, 83, 85

I

if/then reasoning 58
ignoring the question (fallacy) 63–4
implicit categories (in syllogisms) 38
induction (inductive reasoning) 31–5, 37, 62, 73
inductive leap 32

interdisciplinary research topics 94–5
invalid (syllogisms) 43, 45–7, 49–50, 52
issue 8, 9, 11, 12, 15, 17–18, 61, 63–5,
    96, 97, 98–100, 101
  in an outline 98–100, 101

J

"Jabberwocky" (Carroll) 52–4
jumping to conclusions *see* hasty
    generalization (fallacy)

K

King, Martin Luther Jr 73, 74

L

"laws" of science 31
lesser of two evils 67
  see also faulty dilemma (fallacy)
librarian 21–2, 25, 29, 97
literary techniques 21–2, 29
logic, Aristotelian *see* Aristotle
logos 73–4
"Love is a Fallacy" (Shulman) 75, 76–86

M

Macbeth 64
"Magic 8" challenge 4
major premise *see* premise, major
major proposition *see* proposition, major
manuscript 103–5
Marlow, Christopher 75, 86–7
Marvell, Andrew 90–1
matters of taste 10, 13, 86, 106
media 28, 61
media center 21, 97, 102, 104
media specialist 22, 29, 97, 102
metacognition 6–8
metaphor 34–5, 89, 91
.mil *see* domains (network)
minor premise *see* premise, major
minor proposition *see* proposition, minor
Modern Languages Association (MLA) 22,
    98, 103, 104
mutually exclusive 56

N

network domains *see* domains (network)
non sequitur (fallacy) 66
note cards 22
"The Nymph's Reply to the Shepherd"
    (Raleigh) 75, 88–9

O

old information 25–6
online information 21–2, 23, 29, 102–3
opinion 2, 10, 21, 24, 28, 29–30, 69, 70,
    74, 98, 103, 104
  see also appeal to popular opinion (fallacy)
opposition 11, 22, 47, 64, 69, 75,
    93, 100, 101
.org *see* domains (network)
organization 3, 4–5, 22, 28, 30, 97,
    98, 102, 105
  organization challenge 4–5
organizing evidence *see* evidence, organizing

P

parade of horrors (fallacy) 67
"The Passionate Shepherd to His Love"
    (Marlowe) 75, 87
peer-reviewed sources *see* sources;
    peer-reviewed
periodicals 24
persuasive outline forms
  by pros/cons 99–100
  by issues 101–2
pity *see* appeal to pity (fallacy)
plain folks (appeal) 69
poisoning the well 69, 83–4, 86
  see also ad hominem (fallacy)
popular opinion *see* appeal to popular
    opinion (fallacy)
pork (pork barrel spending) 16
post hoc/propter hoc (fallacy) 65–6
precision in language 39
premise 12, 47, 66
  contradictory 66, 81
  major 17–9, 29, 46, 48, 58, 63, 67, 98
  minor 17–9, 28–30, 46, 98
propaganda (propagandists) 22, 61
processing 3, 6, 7, 40, 49–51, 62, 66, 86

processing skills challenge 5–6
proposition 11, 12, 13–16, 17–19, 21,
    62–3, 74, 93–4, 96, 98–102, 104
  characteristics of 13–16
  major 17–18, 28
  minor 17
  see also premise

Q

qualifiers 75
question (defined) 13

R

Raleigh, Sir Walter 75, 87, 88
reason 1–2, 76, 88
reasoning
  by classes 37, 40
  deductive see deduction (deductive
    reasoning)
  by either/or see either/or reasoning
  errors in see fallacies
  good vs. bad 43, 45
  by if/then see if/then reasoning
  inductive see induction (inductive
    reasoning)
  syllogistic see syllogisms
red herring 64
reliable source see sources; reliable
research 10, 11, 17, 21–9, 97
  project 93–105 (checklist 104–5;
    evaluation 105; rubric 127)
  responsibility 103
rider (in legislation) 16
"right" and "wrong" 7, 11
  see also valid (syllogisms); invalid
    (syllogisms)
Rogerian argument see Rogers, Carl R.
Rogers, Carl R. 2, 74–5

S

Shakespeare, William 64
Shulman, Max 76
simile 34–5
slippery slope (fallacy) 67
  see also parade of horrors (fallacy)
"some" (in syllogisms) 32, 39, 51
sources
  peer-reviewed 22, 25, 29
  reliable 22–6, 28, 70, 97

special interest group 23
stacking the deck see card stacking
straw man (fallacy) 64
syllogisms
  explanation of 40–1, 45, 46–7
  practice 43, 51, 52–3, 54–55
  in political arguments 55–6

T

testimonial, authority by see authority
Through the Looking Glass (Carroll) 53
topic selection 93–4
  list 94–5
Toulmin, Stephen 2, 75
Toulmin model see Toulmin, Stephen
"To His Coy Mistress" 90
"To the Virgins, to Make Much of Time"
    (Herrick) 75, 89
transference, authority by see authority
triangulating evidence 28, 30, 97
"true" 46, 47, 51
tu quoque (fallacy) 70

U

unqualified generalization see
    generalization

V

valid (syllogisms) 42–3, 46–7, 50–1, 56
validity, tests for 33, 43, 46–7, 54–5
Venn diagrams 37–40
  working with 41–6
verifiable evidence 24
  see also sources
verifiable facts 10, 13, 29, 47
vertical files 22
voice of authority see authority

W

The Wall Street Journal 24
warrants 75
Weather Bureau 24

Y

"you too" (fallacy) see tu quoque (fallacy)

www.ingramcontent.com/pod-product-compliance
Ingram Content Group UK Ltd.
Pitfield, Milton Keynes, MK11 3LW, UK
UKHW041919140426
5217IPUK00013B/237